TRANCE

JORGE LUIS ALVAREZ PUPO

PERCEVAL PRESS

This book is dedicated to my mother,

Angela, my father, Pascual, and

my grandmother Rosa Castell.

I would like to thank, in a very special

way, Viggo Mortensen and Pilar Perez.

For the production scans of the book,

my thanks go to Humberto Mayol, and for

the design I thank Michele Perez. Thanks also to

Lourdes Socarras, director of the Fototeca

de Cuba, and to all the people who work

there, as well as all the people who,

at least once, trusted me.

Este libro es dedicado a mi

madre Angela, mi padre Pascual,

y mi abuela Rosa Castell.

Quisiera dar las gracias, en

una manera muy especial,

a Viggo Mortensen y Pilar Perez.

Por la producción de scans del libro

mis gracias a Humberto Mayol y por el

diseño a Michele Perez. Gracias también a

Lourdes Socarras, Director de Fototeca de

Cuba y a todas las personas empleadas allí;

incluyendo también a todas las personas,

aunque sea una vez, confiaron en mí.

TRANCE

ISBN 0-9721436-6-1
© 2003 Perceval Press
© 2003 All images Jorge Luis Alvarez Pupo
All rights reserved, including the right of
reproduction in whole or in part in any form.

Limited edition of 1,000 copies

Published by Perceval Press
1223 Wilshire Blvd., Suite F
Santa Monica, CA 90403
www.percevalpress.com

Editors: Pilar Perez and Viggo Mortensen
Design: Michele Perez
Copy Editor: Sherri Schottlaender

Printed in Spain at Jomagar, S/A

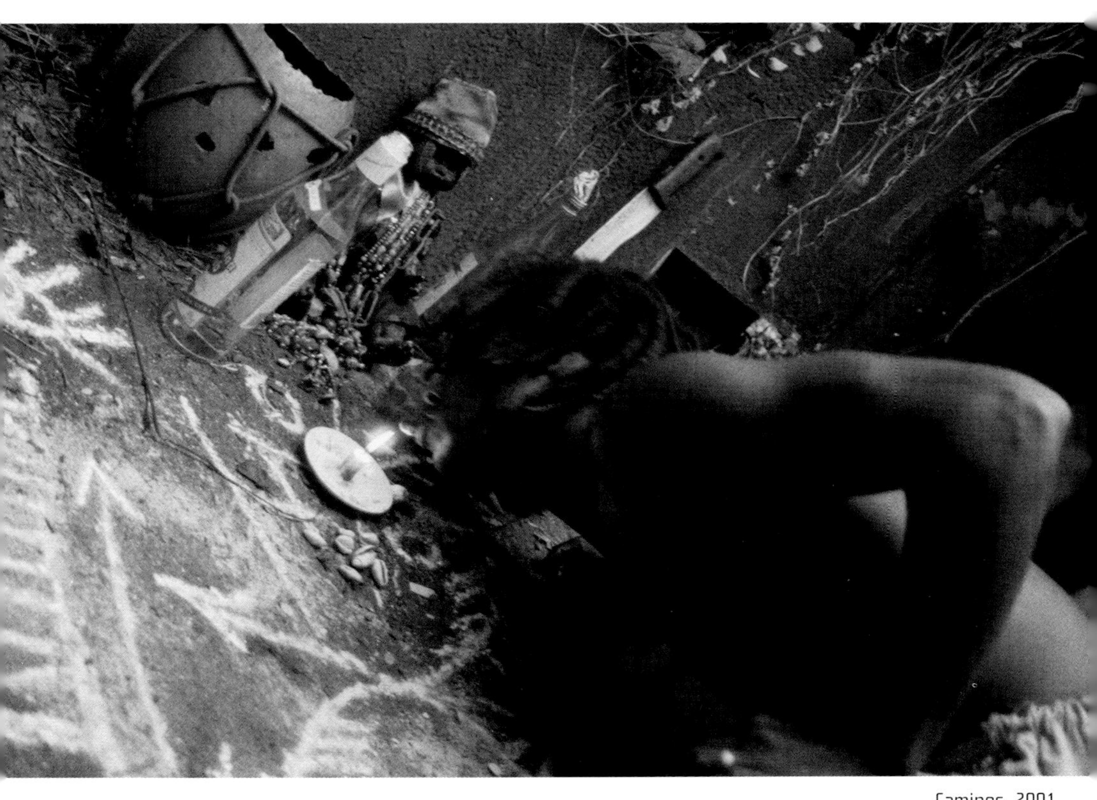

Caminos, 2001

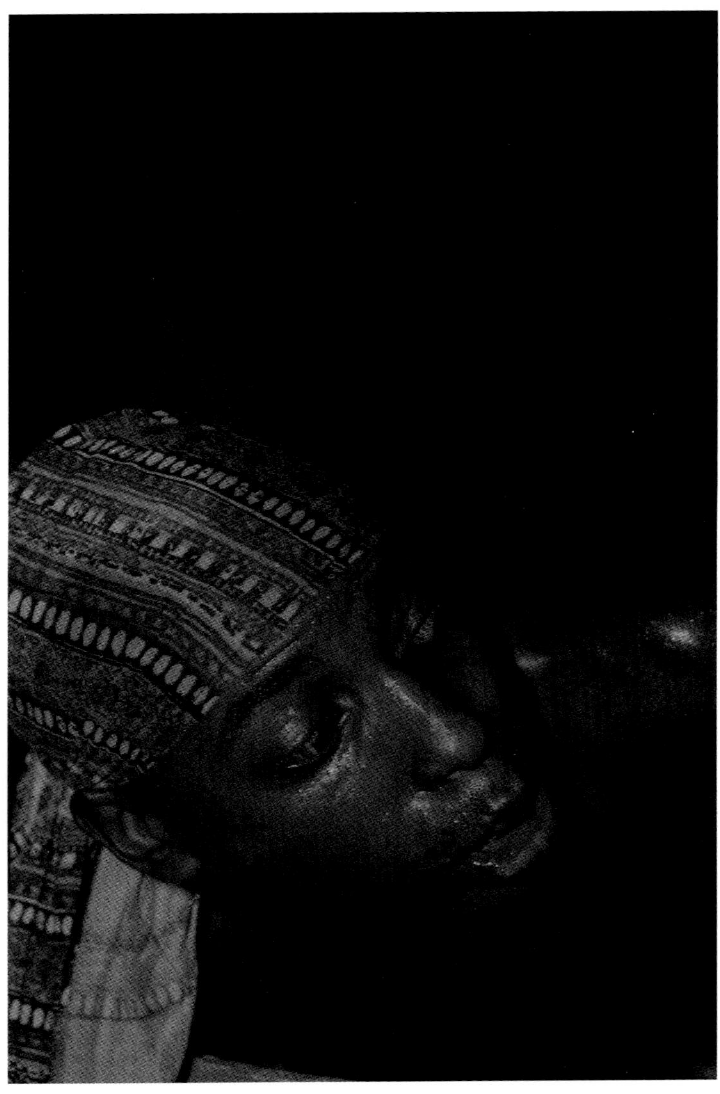

Sin título, 1999

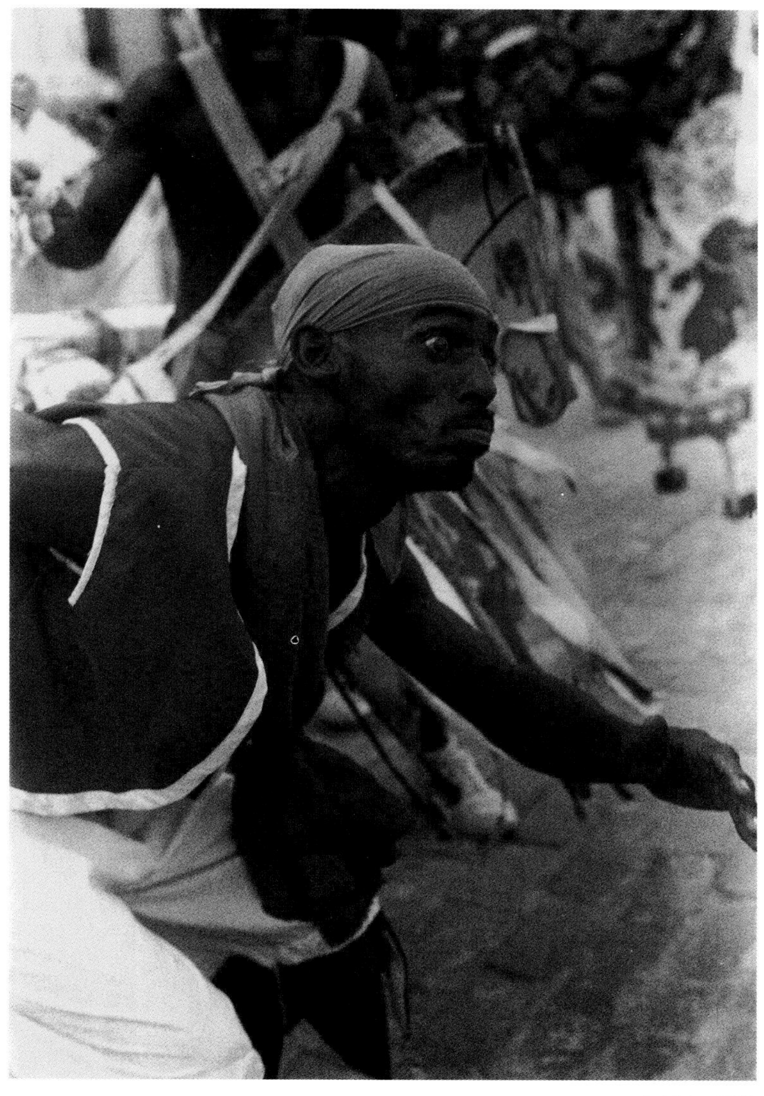

Cabildo, 2000

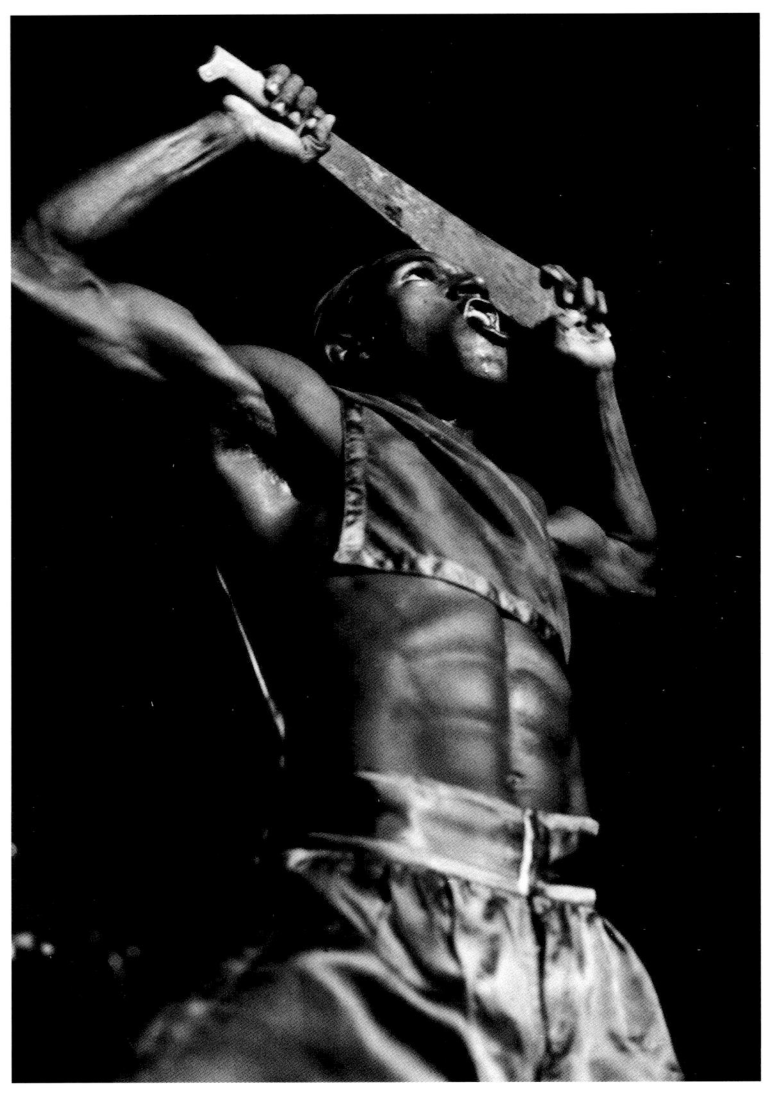

Grito de libertad, 1999

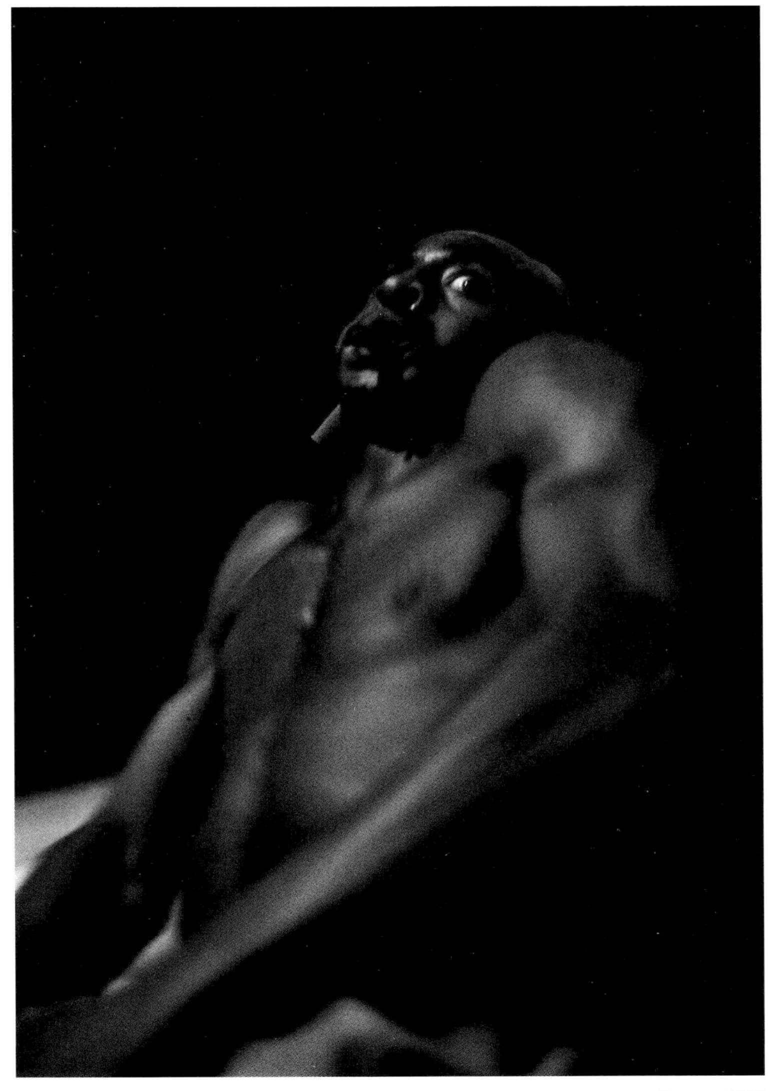

Trance, 1999

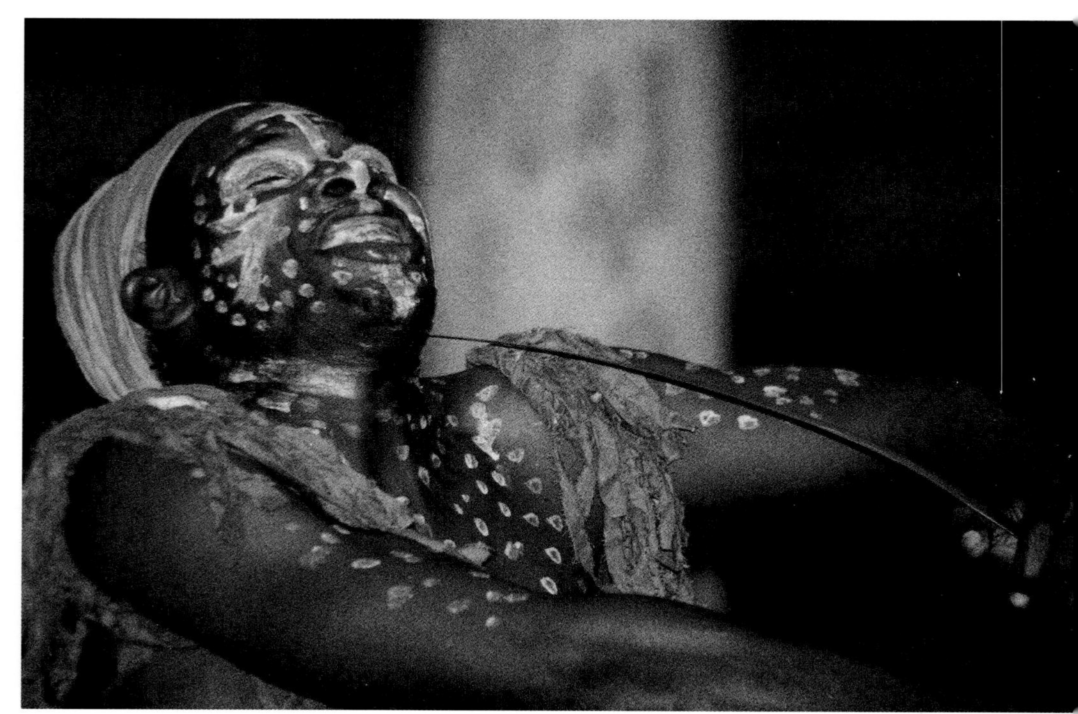

Sin título, 2001

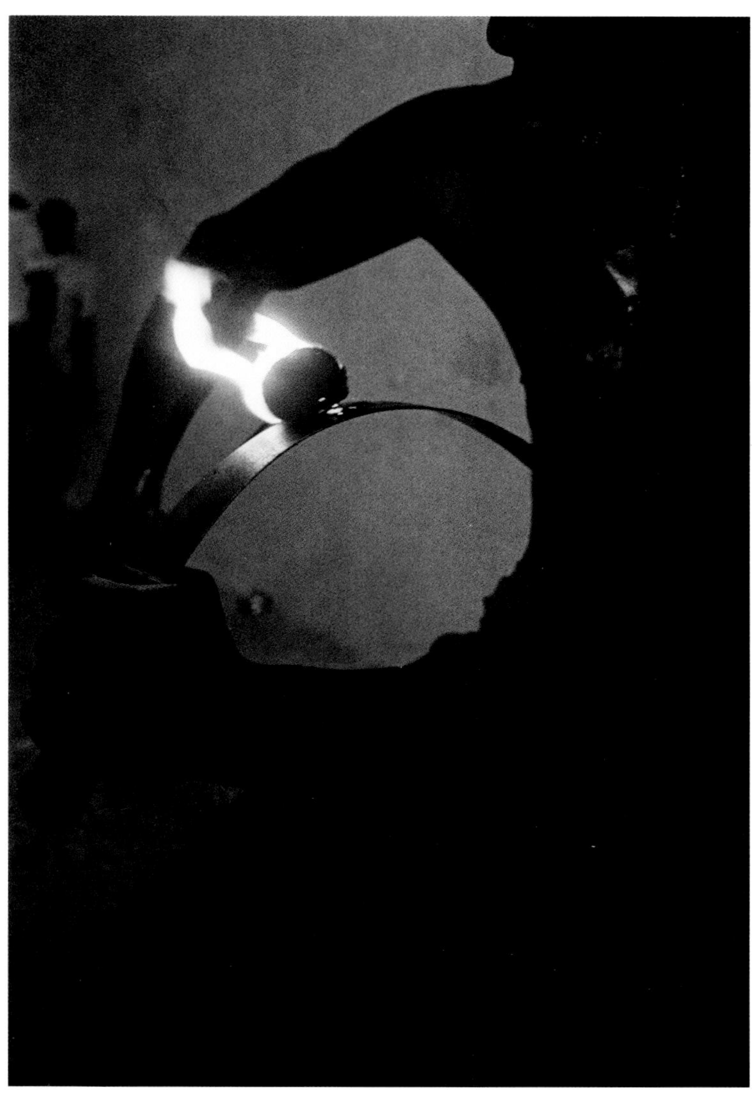

Sin título, 2001

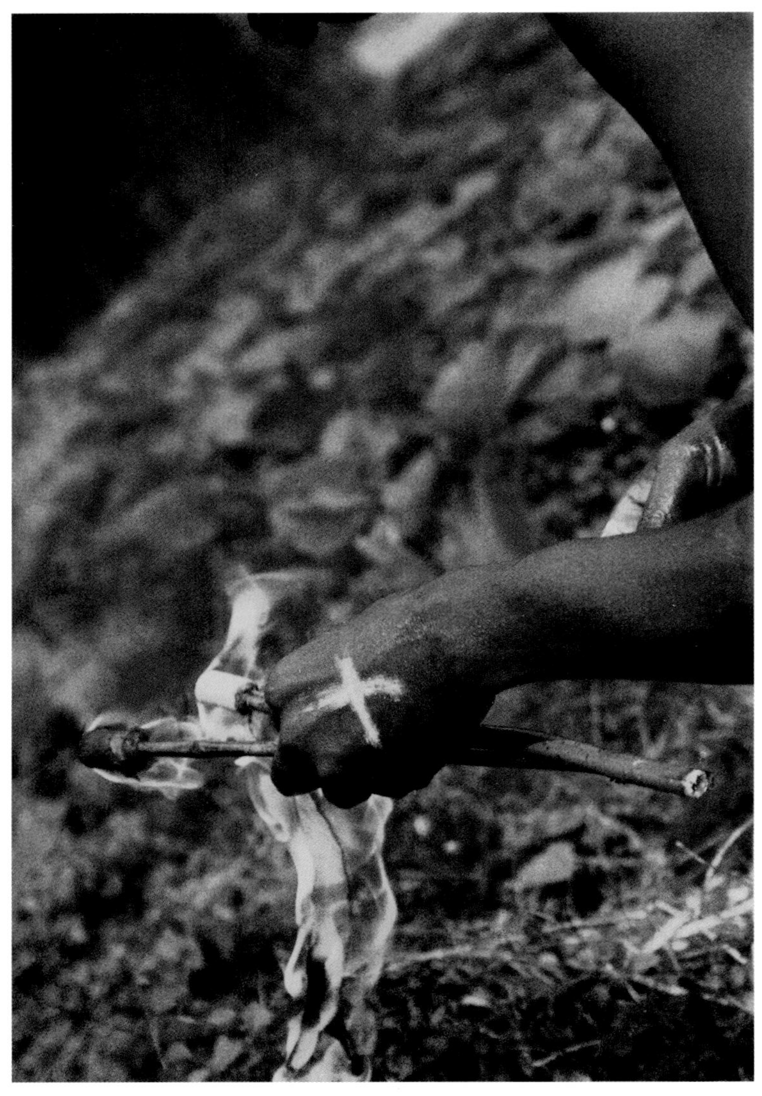

Sin título, 2003

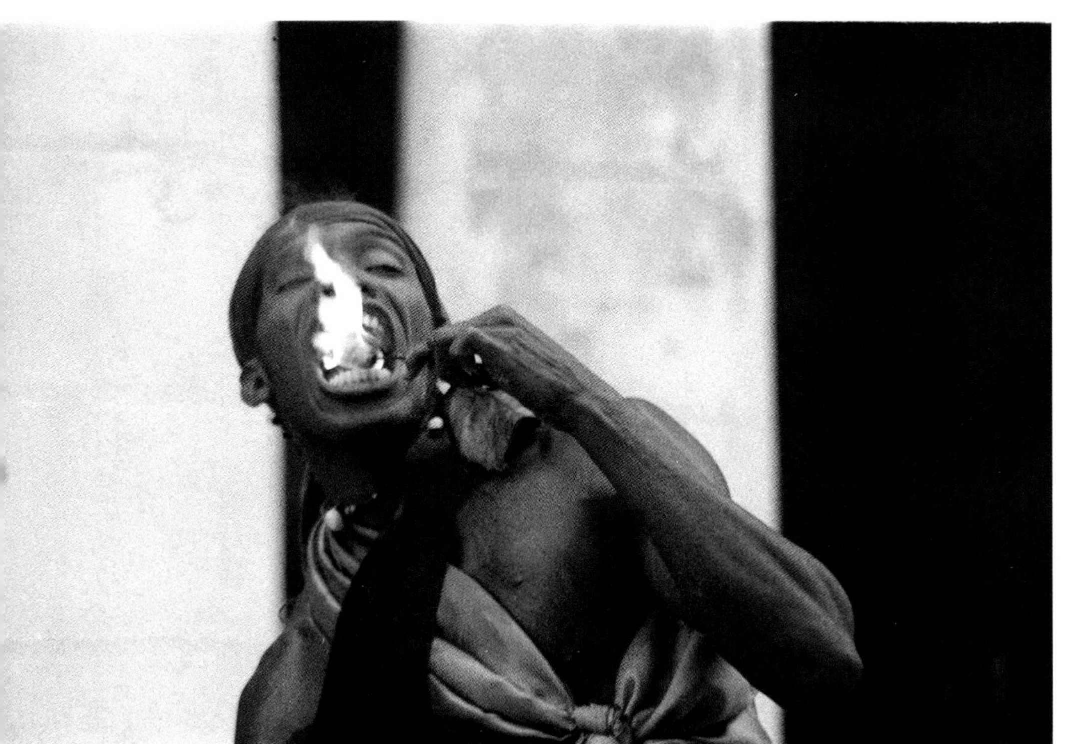

Sin título, 2001

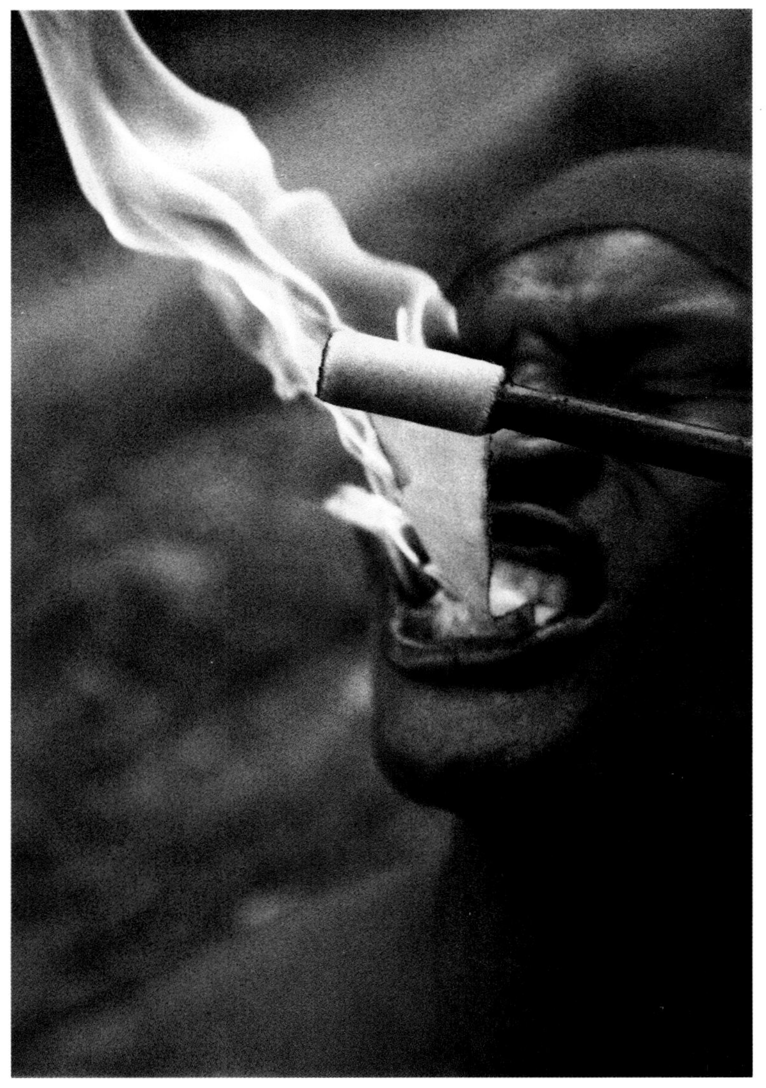

Sin título, 2003

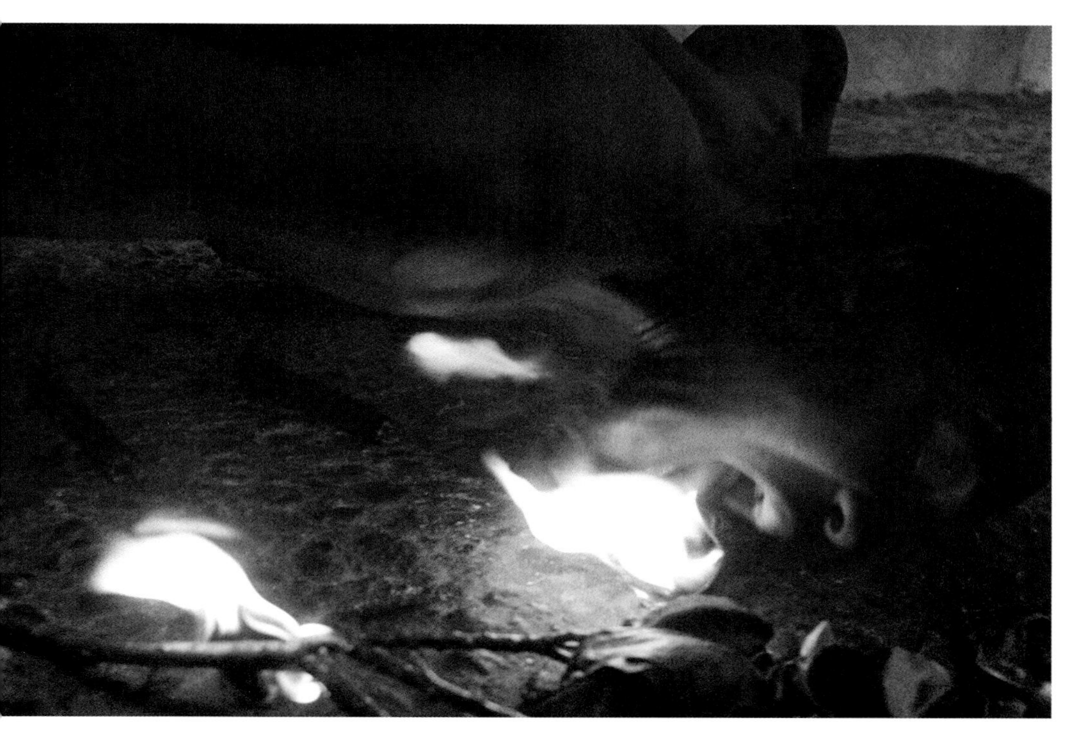

Sin título, 2000

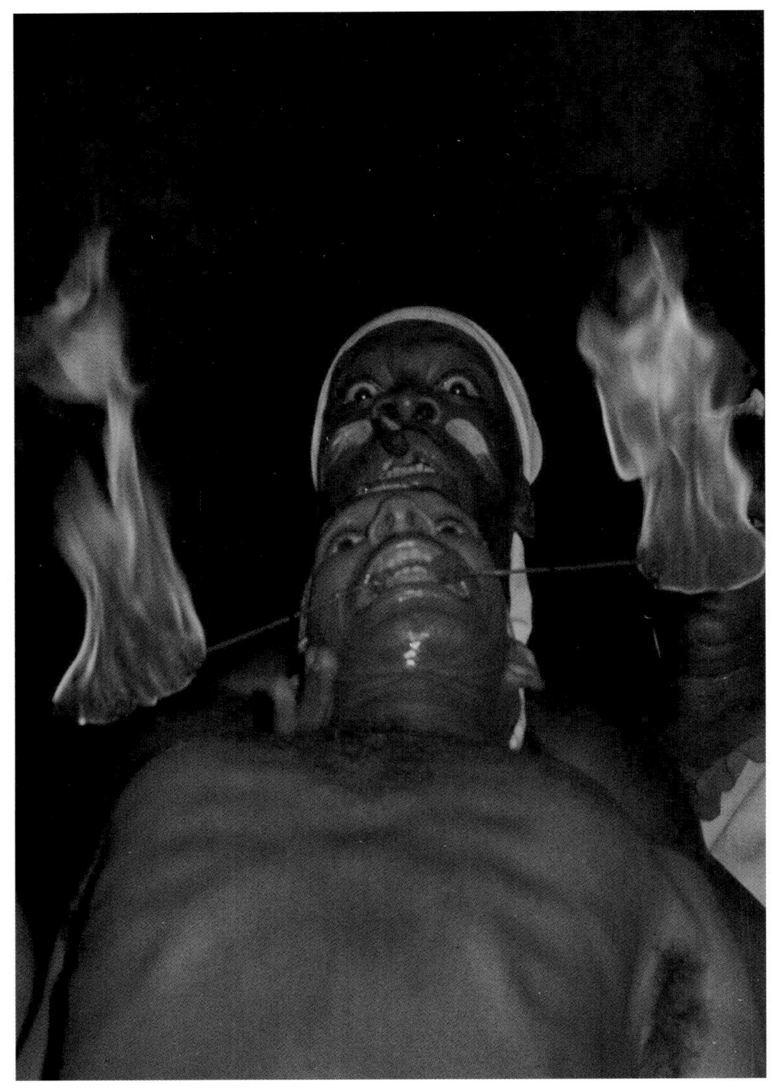

Sin título, 1999

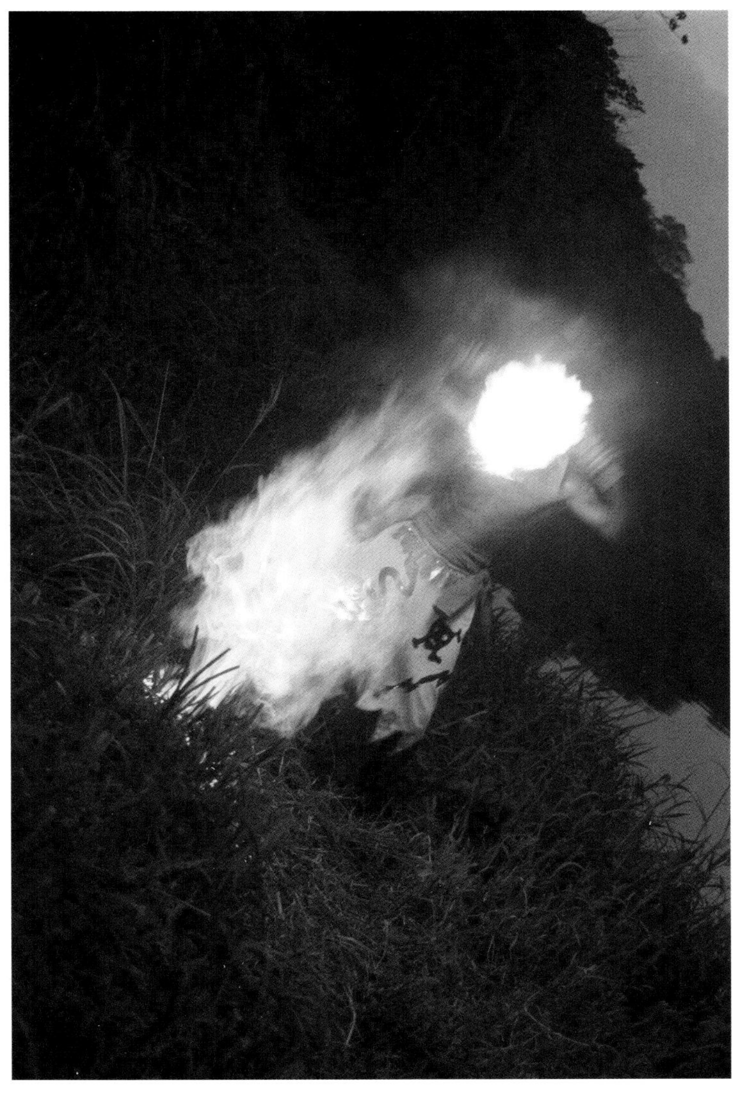

Sin título, 2002

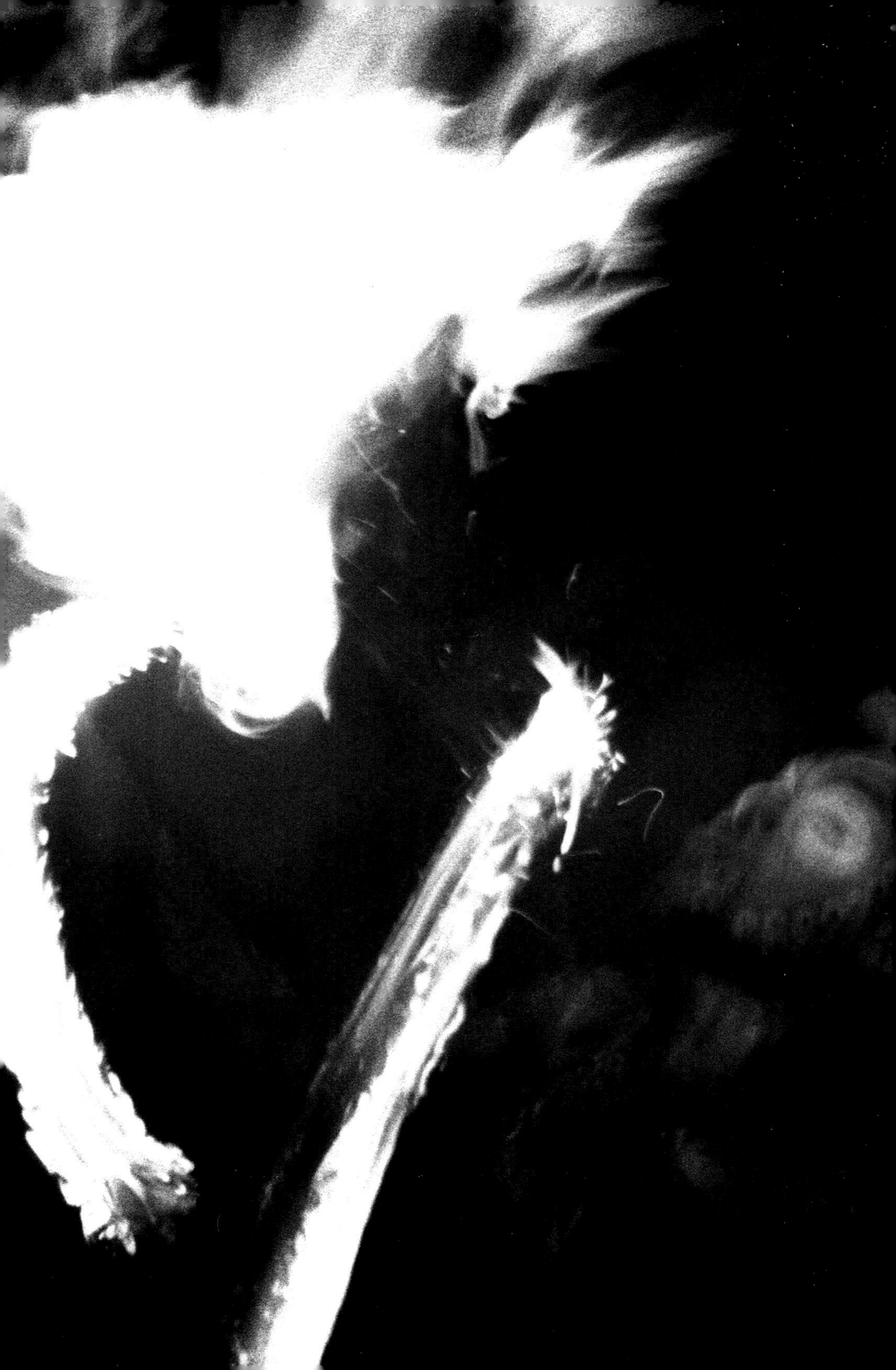

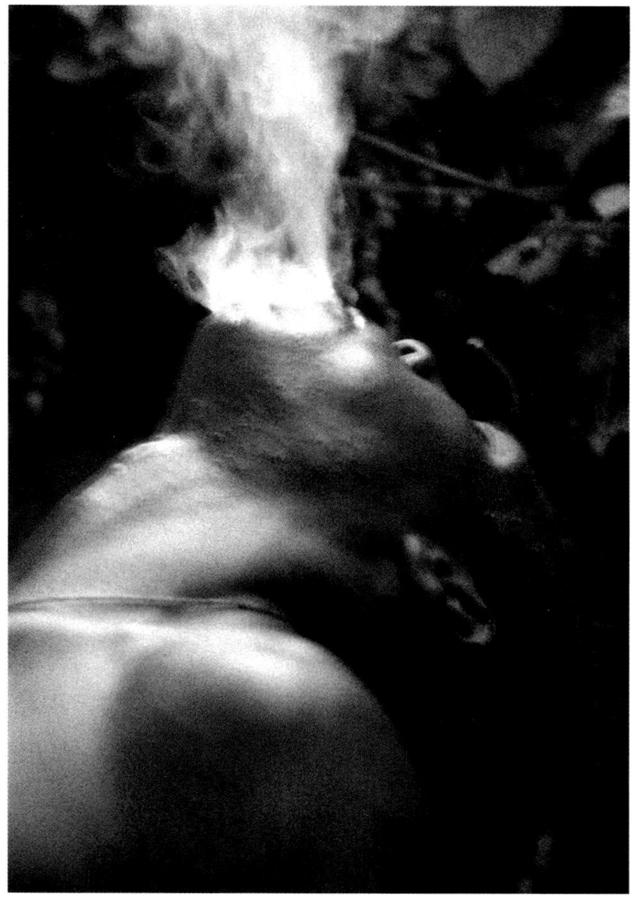

Sin título, 2002

The world of life experiences that a work of art is capable of evoking is often more important than the work of art itself. "It bothers me sometimes that it is only art objects that monopolize and define our interest in the artistic. Works of art are always emanations, consequences, and effects whose center of irradiation is never other than the human, the individual, the artist," art critic Orlando Hernández has said, making manifest an emphatic denial of the separation between art and life.

Artist Jorge Luis Alvarez Pupo constructs in his work a universe created out of the rituals of faith employed by human beings to access the spiritual world. The images that appear in Pupo's photographs are always linked in each viewer's mind to the chain of his or her own experiences and memories. The works speak to the manner in which individuals have developed their own mystical side, their inner self, beliefs, or faith—if not with prayers and rites, then with ideas, hopes, or "visions." Each person is molded by religion as well as the collective unconscious that defines the cultural context of Cuba, where those who are not practitioners nevertheless cannot avoid everyday contact with the religious or spiritual.

In the black-and-white photographs that Pupo brings out of the penumbra of the darkroom, images of humans appear as they emerge from the shadows,

El mundo de vivencias que es capaz de despertar una obra de arte es muchas veces más importante que la obra misma. "A veces me molesta que sean solo las obras quienes monopolicen y definan nuestro interés por lo artístico. Las obras de arte son siempre emanaciones, consecuencias, efectos, cuyo centro de irradiación nunca es otro que el hombre, el individuo, el artista" expresaría el crítico de arte Orlando Hernández, haciendo manifiesto un particular rechazo hacia esta separación entre vida y obra.

Y el artista Jorge Luis Alvarez Pupo construye una obra - universo formada por los rituales de fe que el ser humano realiza para acceder al mundo de lo espiritual. Las imágenes que aparecen en sus fotografías son siempre completadas en la mente del espectador por la cadena de su propia experiencia y recuerdos, por la manera en que este halla desarrollado su parte mística e interior, su creencia o fe—si no con ritos o rezos con pensamientos, anhelos o "visiones", o simplemente con la idea que cada uno se forma de lo religioso a partir de ese inconsciente colectivo que define el contexto cultural de nuestro país, donde quien no es practicante no puede evitar el cotidiano contacto indirecto—El arte así nos remite abiertamente a la vida.

En las impresiones de blanco y negro que Pupo va trabajando en el laboratorio y sacando en la penumbra del cuarto

like the first rays of light. These photographs recall the Santería creation story, with Oloddumare creating nature and living beings by snatching them from the dark kingdom of Echu. Revealed in Pupo's works are men who struggle against the elements in their primitive nakedness, a look of dread evident on their faces as they confront the powers of fire, shadows, and destiny. The photographic series "Los poderes de Oggu" (The powers of Oggu) captures in an extraordinary manner the way in which men battle steel and fire—elements that identify the Loa—or dominate them as possessions.

Pupo also creates a photographic document that explicates the cultural roots of Cuba, but he does not pretend to be an anthropologist: rather than staying coldly removed from people's professions of faith, he instead allows himself to be absorbed by spiritual beliefs and the feelings that drive them—fear, vulnerability, love, sadness, or hate. The cold documentarian is replaced by the passionate witness.

Pupo differs from the researchers who begin their work with scientific detachment but eventually come to believe in the worldview of their subjects; he is already familiar with Cuban religions, having been born in Guanabacoa and living currently in Regla—both cities are Cuban religious centers—and having a long association with Santería (Regla de Ocho), and with voodoo, which has fewer practi-

oscuro, aparecen las imágenes de los seres humanos que emergen de las sombras con los primeros haces de luz, como hiciera Oloddumare cuando creó la naturaleza y los seres vivientes, arrebatándolos a la oscuridad del reino de ECHU. Aparecen los hombres que luchan contra los elementos en su desnudez primitiva, en los rostros las miradas de pavor por la fuerza de los poderes del fuego, de las sombras y del destino. La serie fotográfica "Los poderes de Oggú", capta de manera extraordinaria la forma en que los hombres se debaten ante el poder del hierro o del fuego—elementos que identifican al loa—o los dominan como posesos.

Pupo crea también un documento científico que nos habla sobre las raíces culturales de Cuba, pero no pretendiendo ser un antropólogo fríamente alejado de las profesiones de fe que la gente realiza. Dejándose llenar de la fuerza espiritual que proporcionan las creencias y los sentimientos que compulsan a ellas: el miedo, la desprotección, el amor, la tristeza o el odio. Dejando al frío documentarista por el apasionado cultor.

Pero Pupo tampoco es el investigador que comienza distanciado y termina convencido por los ritos y cosmovisión del investigado como los científicos que llegan a vivir en las comunidades y terminan "captados" por sus costumbres y religiones, pues Pupo ha nacido en Guanabacoa y vive

tioners in the Cuban territories. It is when Pupo becomes an artist, in search of motivation, that he rediscovers his religious beliefs from a new perspective—from behind the camera.

After many years, Pupo has arrived at the conclusion that these religions are a philosophy about life. The visions of individuals are doors to access the real world: the visions are the true way to "see" what is around us. Divination—the act by which truth is accessed and revealed through seashells or coconuts—allows believers to internalize their faith, creating contact with the gods and contact with nature itself. There is no underestimation of any object, plant, animal, or human: they are all agents inside a universe of actions and protections, agents that embrace or reject from their condition of invisibility. Here is where the phrase "Ver es creer" (Seeing is believing) becomes reality. The ability to see from another perspective is implicit in these works, whose images attempt to seize the unseizable as they portray the invisible—they reveal states of mind more than bodies.

Pupo's elegantly sparse photographs share their simplicity with Santería. In Santería, rituals take place not in grand and opulent cathedrals but in modest homes and towns, important paintings are not created on canvases but rather on the skin of the practitioners of the ceremony,

en Regla, centros religiosos de Cuba, y es desde hace mucho tiempo que se familiariza con la Santería o Regla de Ocho y con el voodoo, una religión menos extendida en el territorio cubano. Es cuando se hace artista, al buscar motivos suficientemente buenos para su arte, que se reencuentra con la religión desde la perspectiva del que observa tras una cámara.

El ha llegado ya desde hace muchos años a la conclusión de que estas religiones son realmente una filosofía de vida donde las visiones que tiene un sujeto en trance son las puertas de acceso al verdadero mundo, la manera real de "ver" lo que nos rodea, las adivinaciones son la forma en que el creyente interioriza su fe como pequeños momentos en que accede a la verdad revelada a través de los caracoles o de los cocos, y su contacto con los dioses es su contacto con la naturaleza misma, puesto que nunca se subestima el menor objeto, planta, animal o humano como agentes dentro de un universo de acciones y protecciones: los agentes que acogen o repelen desde la condición de la invisibilidad. Aquí es donde se hace realidad la sentencia que reza "Ver es Creer", pero ver desde otra perspectiva que lleva implícita estas obras, paradoja de imágenes que tratan de asir lo inasible y de retratar lo invisible, los estados más que los cuerpos.

Las fotografías de Pupo son sencillas como esta religión que no emana de grandes y fastuosas catedrales, sino de casas y barrios humildes, donde

and drawn white lines and circles vibrate with the movement of the arms and faces of the dancers. The beautiful drawings and patterns of voodoo, which are made in the sand, earth, and dust, and later disappear in the wind, are important ephemeral elements of a ceremony rather than long-lasting images.

In his work Pupo captures all forms of movement: the rhythm of dance, the convulsed movements of the possessed who have fallen into a trance, the evolution of a fire's flame, or the manner in which we might imagine that spirits move, as almost imperceptible vibrations that populate the world of the senses.

The series "Visiones" (Visions) is like a gathering of mirages that are not perceived directly with the eyes but rather with some other sense, as when one catches a glimpse of fleeting shadows that disappear when the eye stops. Pupo's photographs in this series capture those immaterial and intangible sensations in such an extraordinary form that everything seems an impossibility seen only by the artist: with his artistic vision, he has captured the moments in a photographic document to convince all unbelievers.

las principales pinturas no son las que se quedan sobre lienzos sino sobre la piel de los practicantes en la ceremonia con líneas y círculos blancos que vibran sobre los brazos y rostros de los que bailan. O como los bellos dibujos y entramados del voodoo que se hacen en arena, tierra o polvo y luego desaparecen con el viento, siendo más importantes como elementos de una ceremonia que como formas que van a perdurar.

Con sus obras, este artista logra captar toda clase de movimientos: el ritmo del baile, los movimientos retorcidos de los poseídos que han caído en trance, las evoluciones de las llamas de un fuego o la forma lenta en que nos imaginamos que se mueven los espíritus, como vibraciones casi imperceptibles que pueblan el mundo sensible.

Y es que toda su serie de "Visiones" es como un conjunto de espejismos que no se perciben directamente con los ojos sino con algún otro sentido. Como cuando al pasar rápido la mirada por algún lugar se adivinan sombras fugaces que luego desaparecen al detener los ojos. Las fotografías de esta serie captan de una manera tan extraordinaria esas sensaciones intangibles e incorpóreas, que todo nos parece un imposible solo visto por el artista y que gracias a un acto inexplicable ha logrado atrapar en el documento fotográfico para convencer a todos los incrédulos.

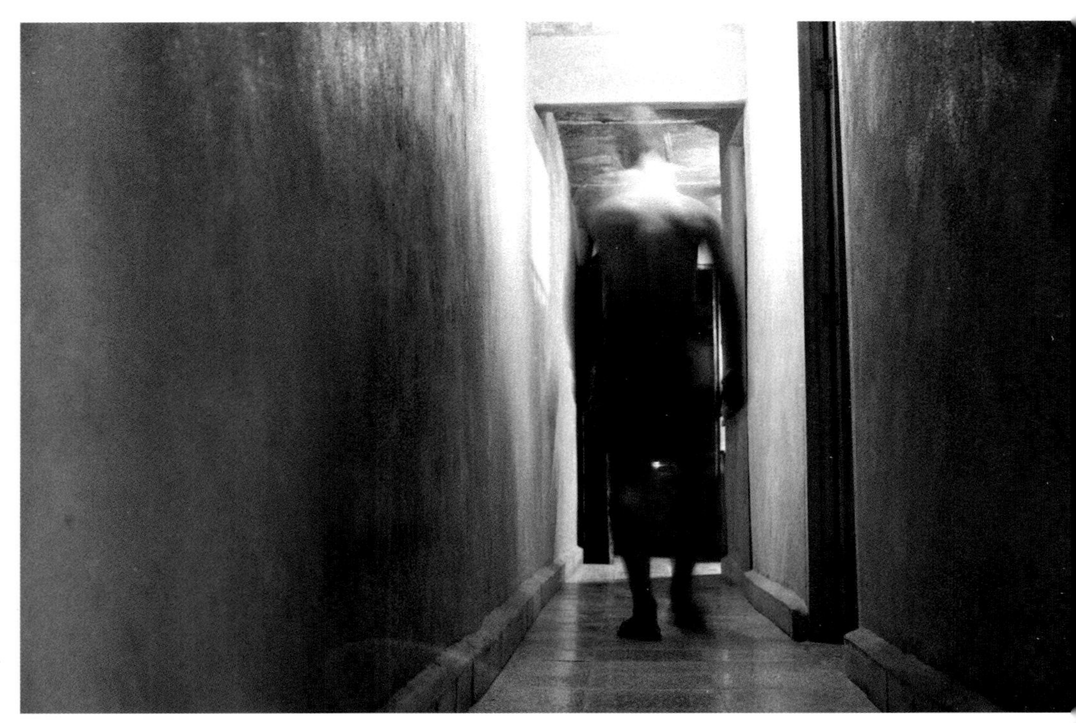

El camino del más allá, 199

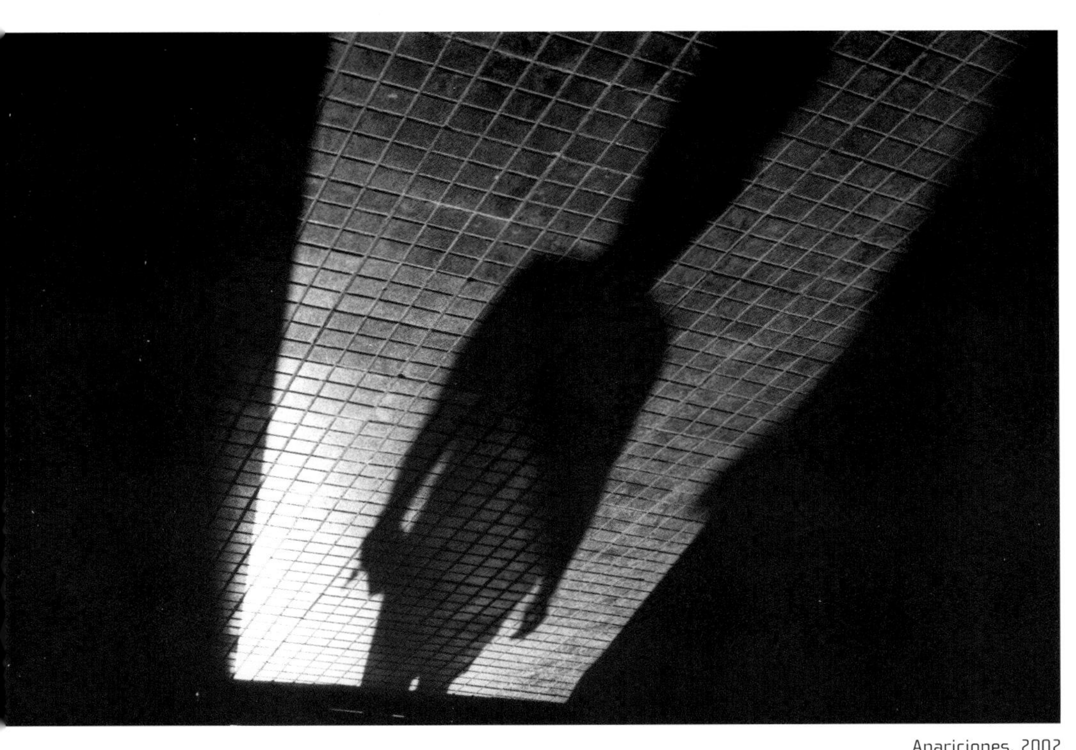

Apariciones, 2002

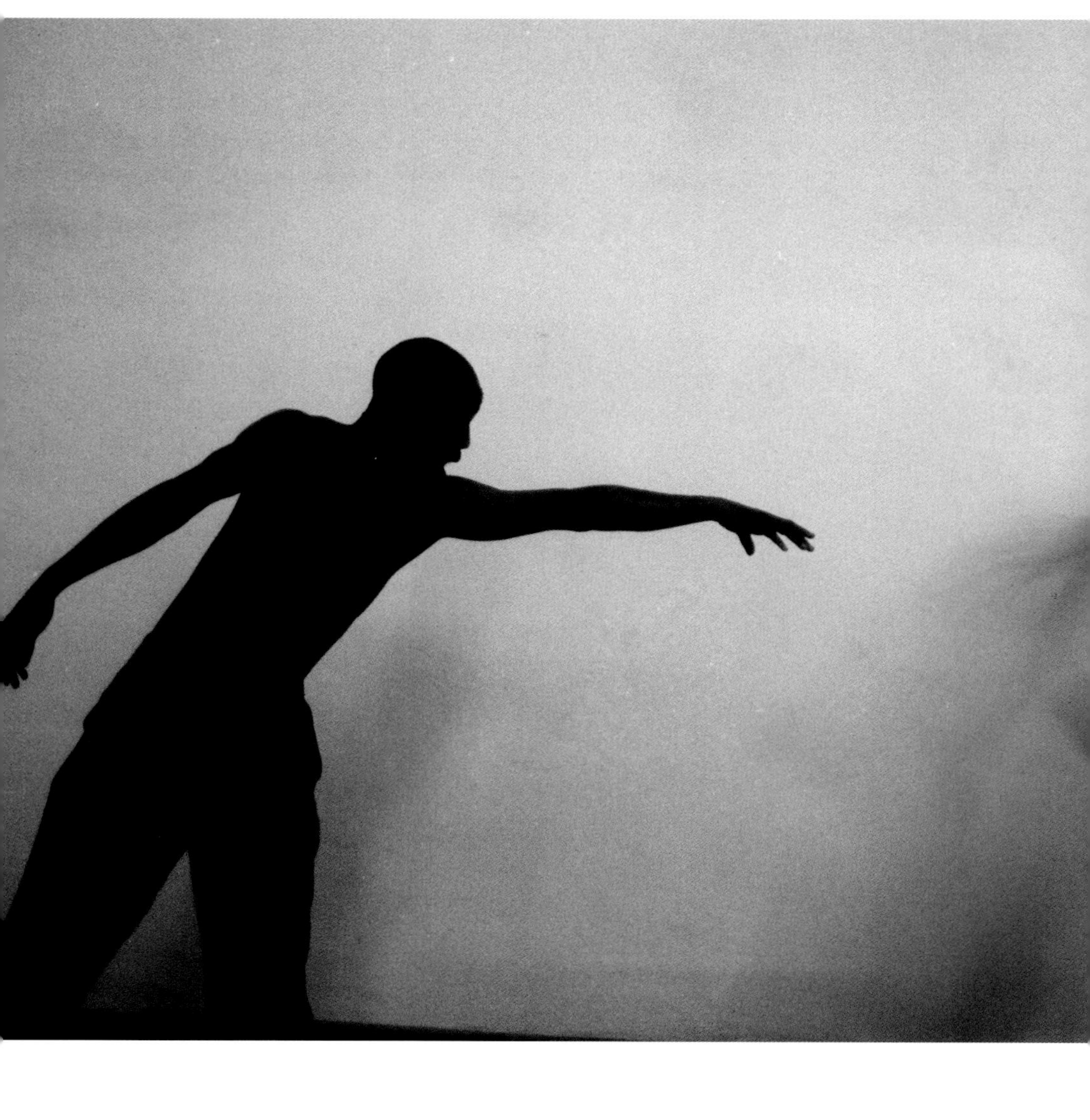

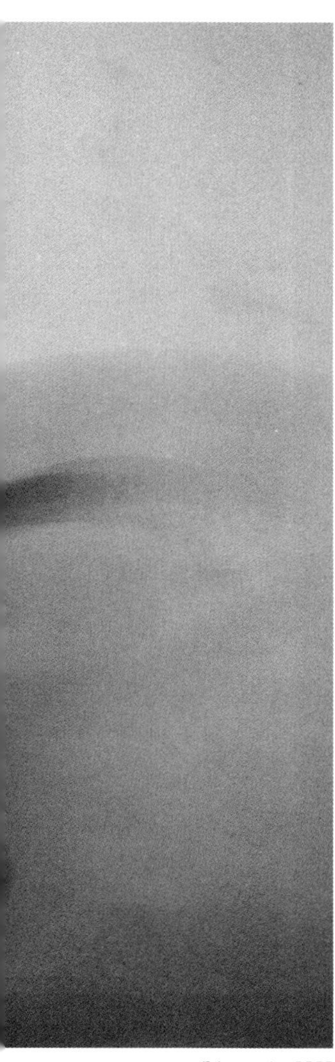

Búsqueda, 2003

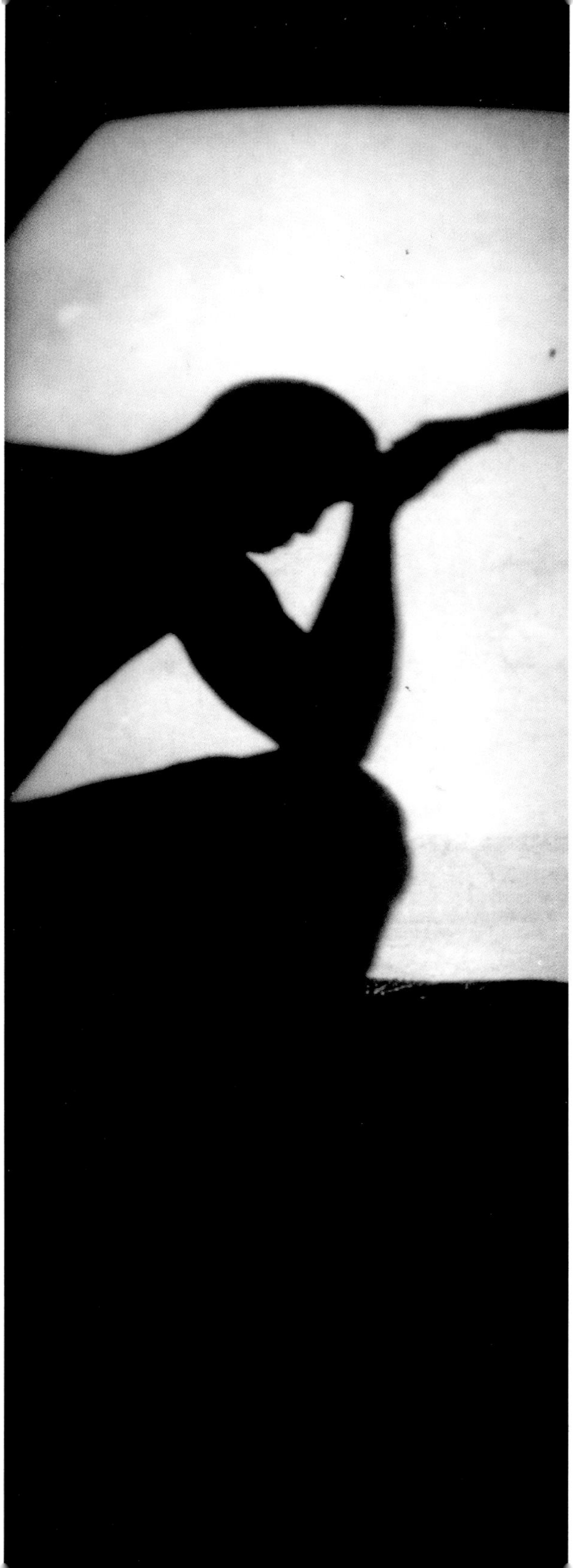

Agonía, 2003

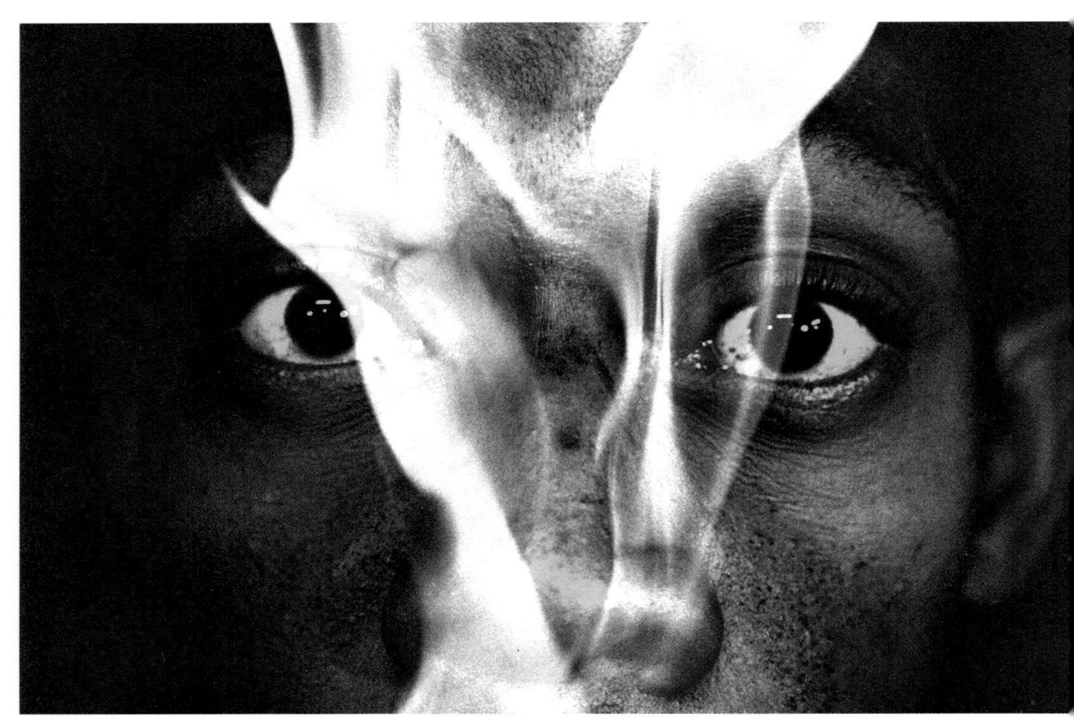

La mirada del diablo, 200

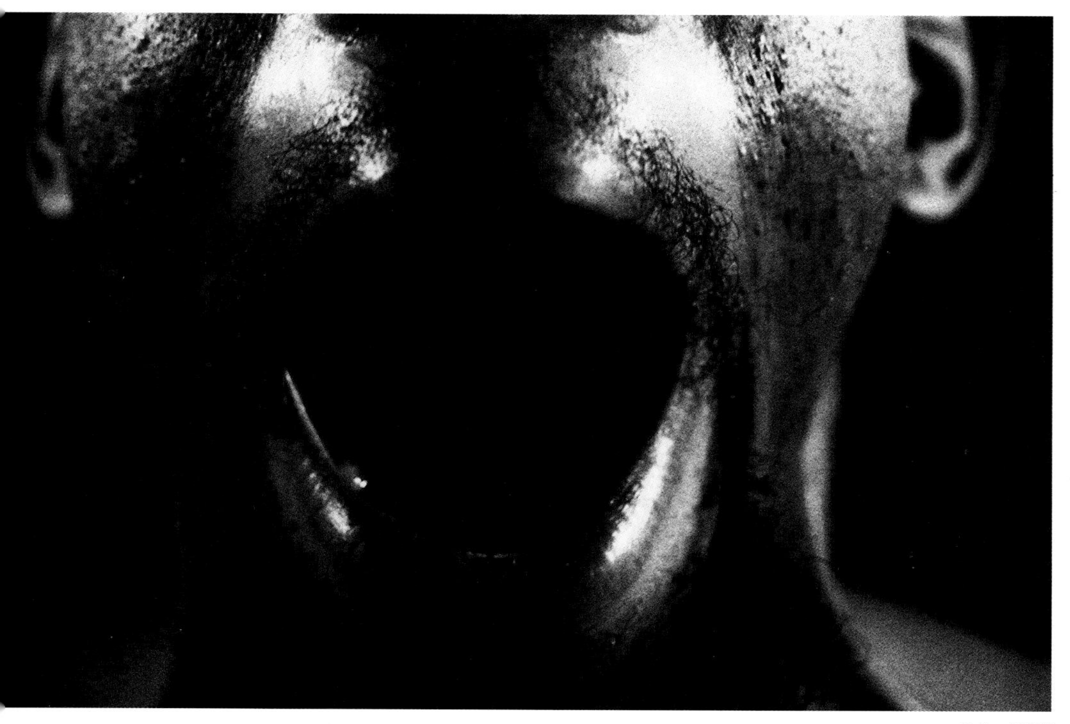

Grito, 2002

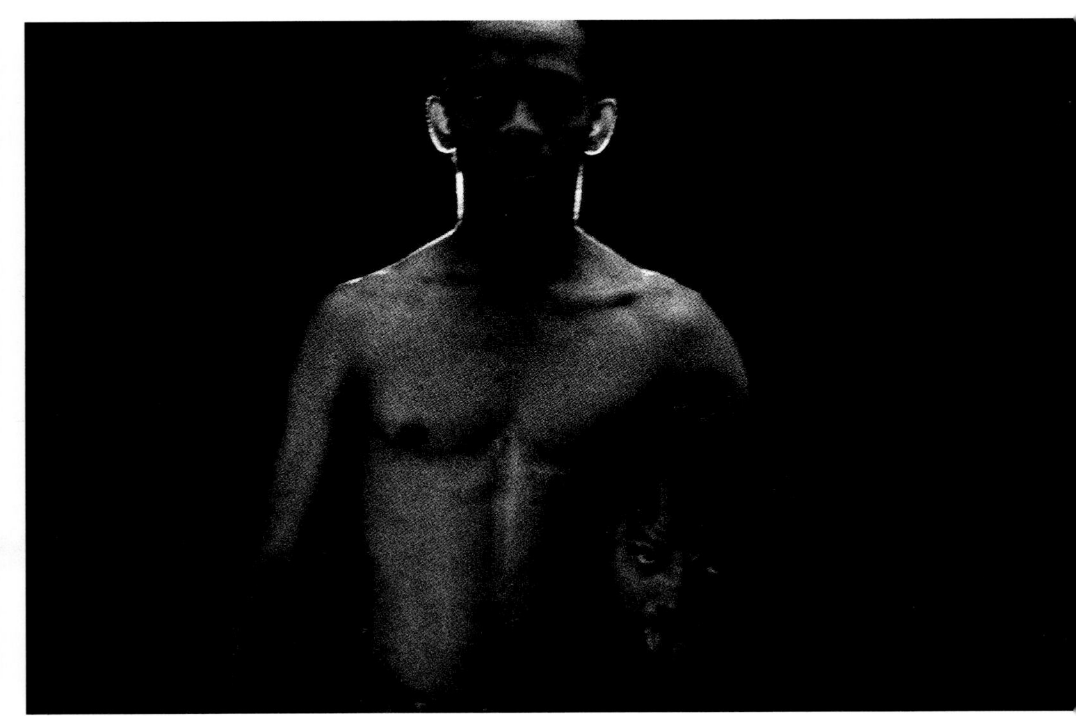

Sin título, 200

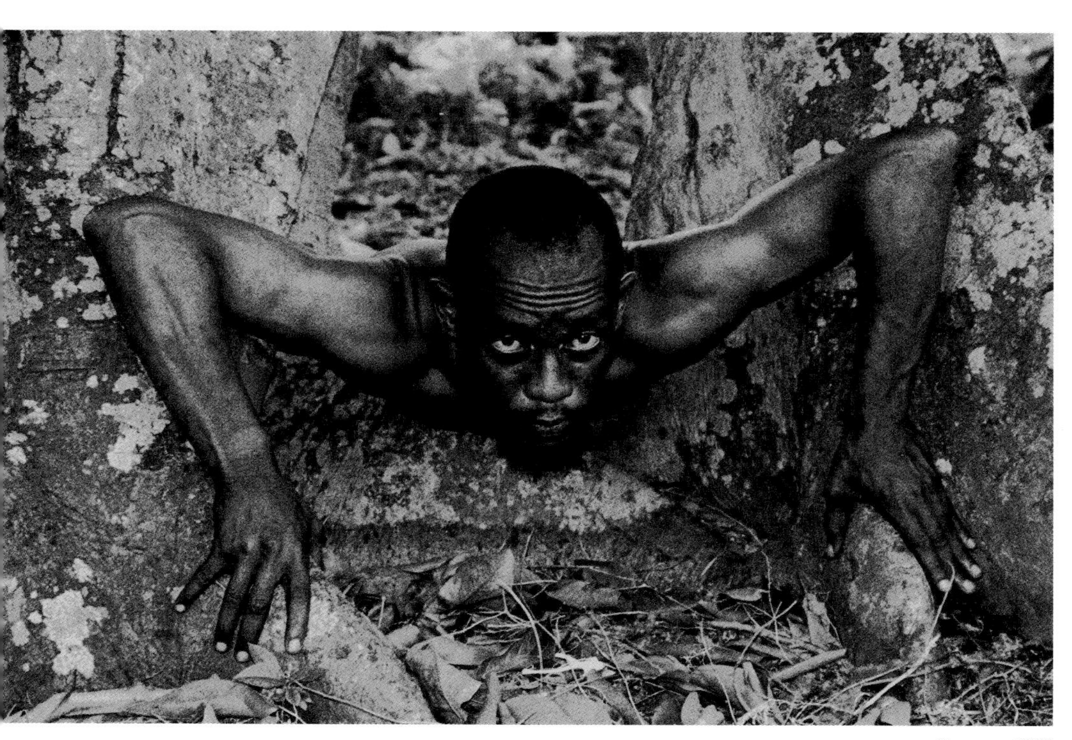

Renacer, 2003

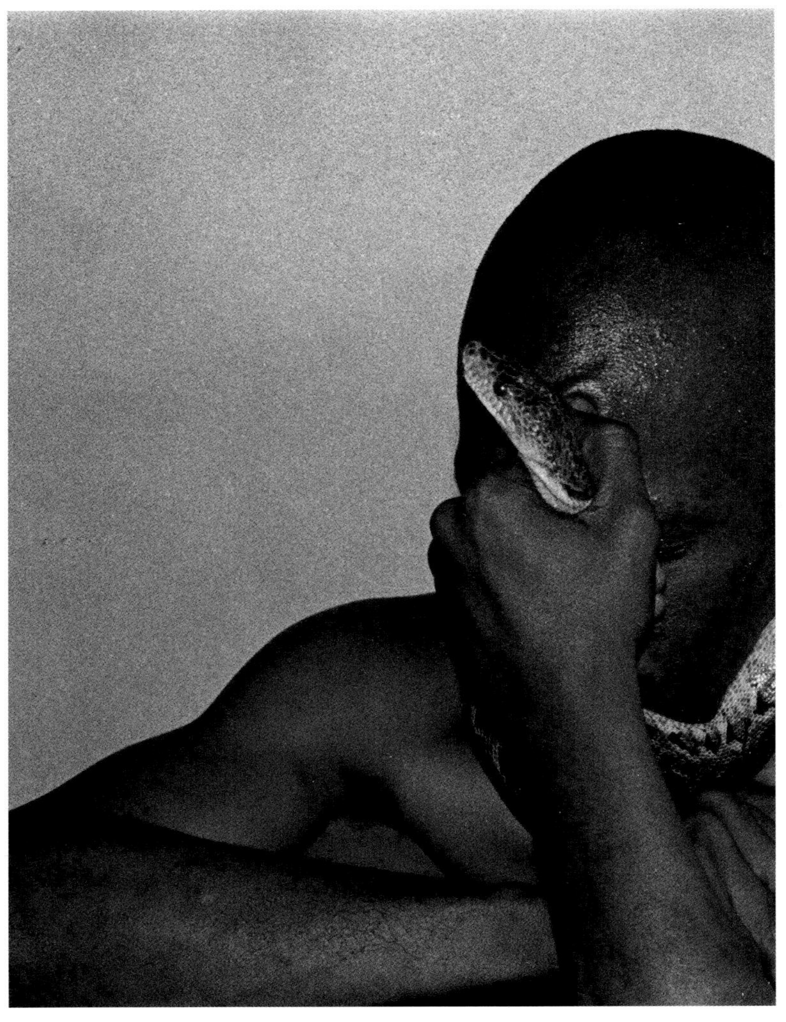

Sin título, 2002

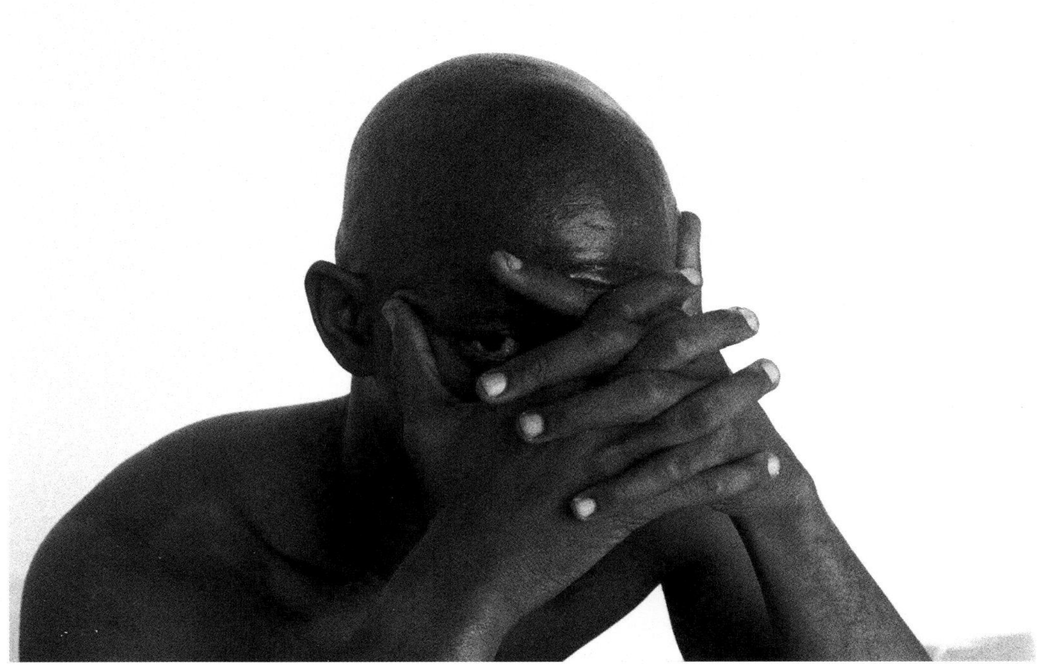

Sin título, 2003

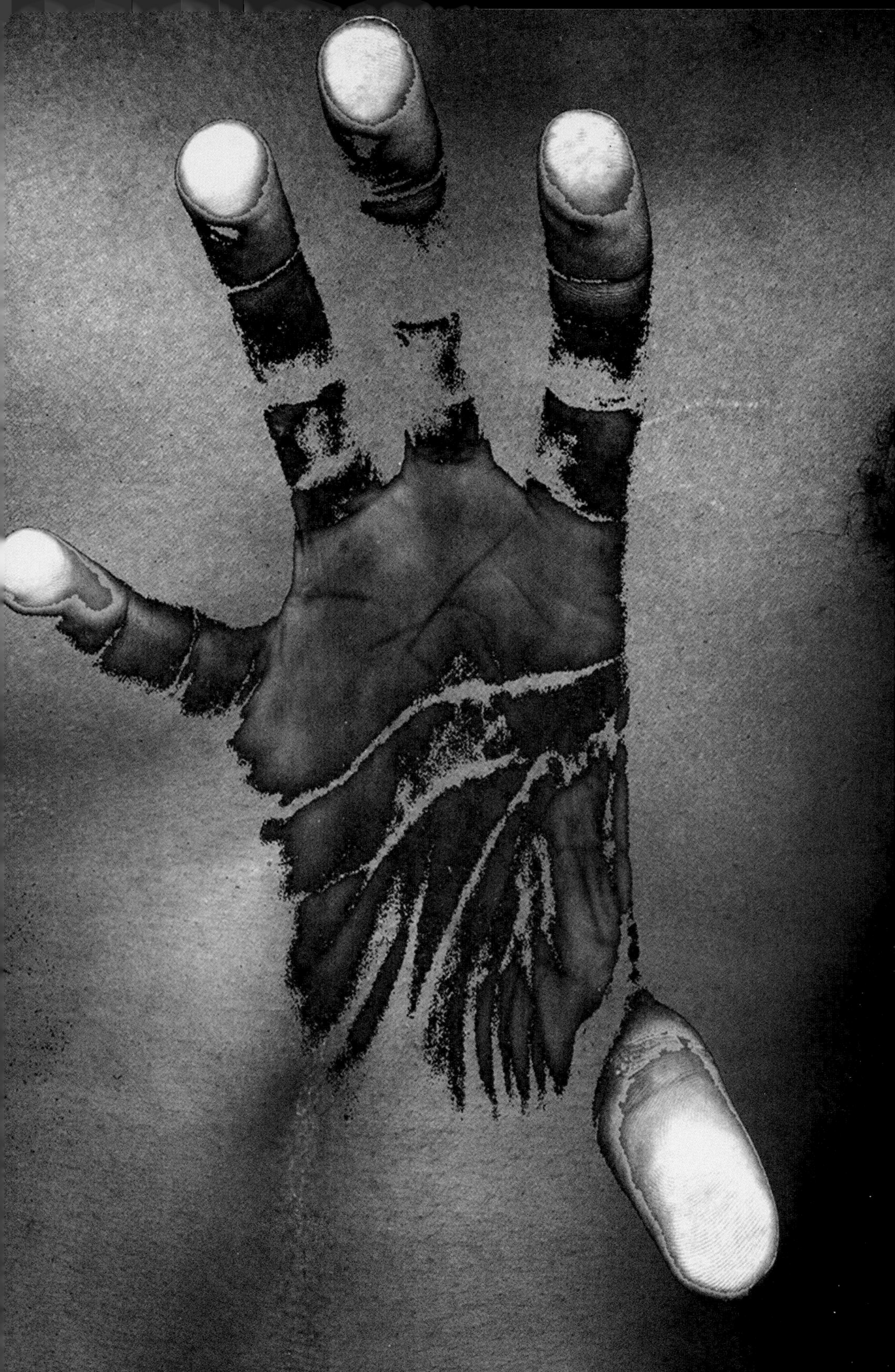

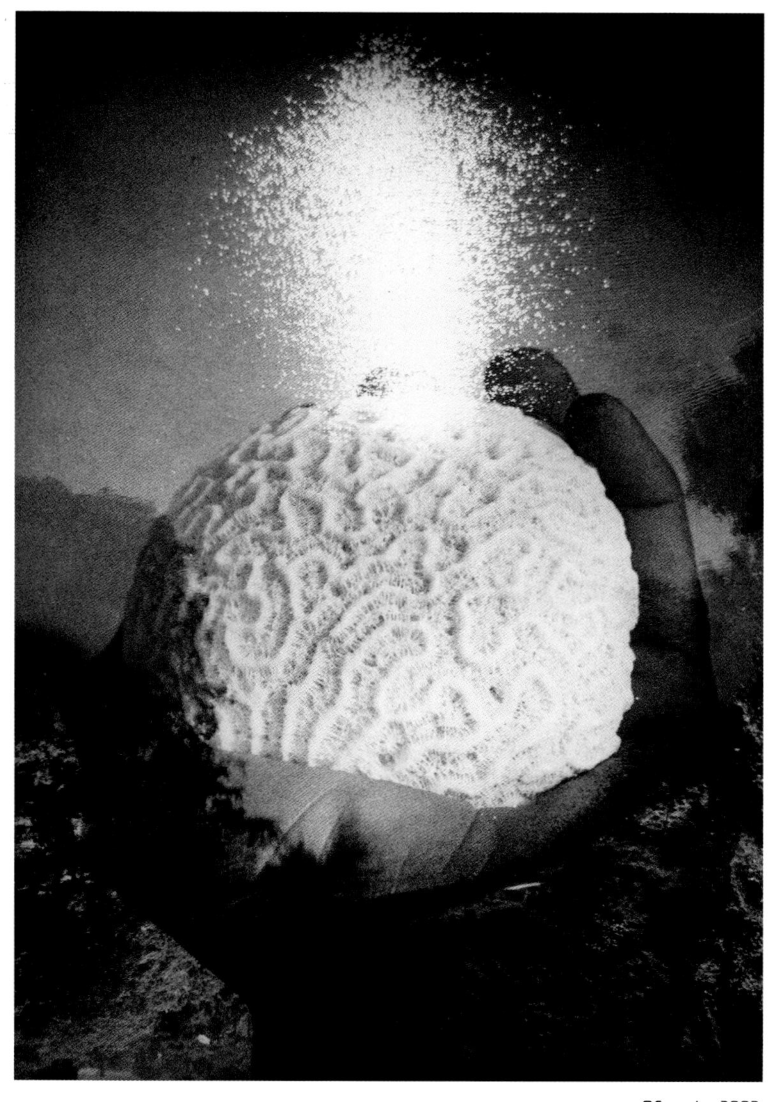

Ofrenda, 2003

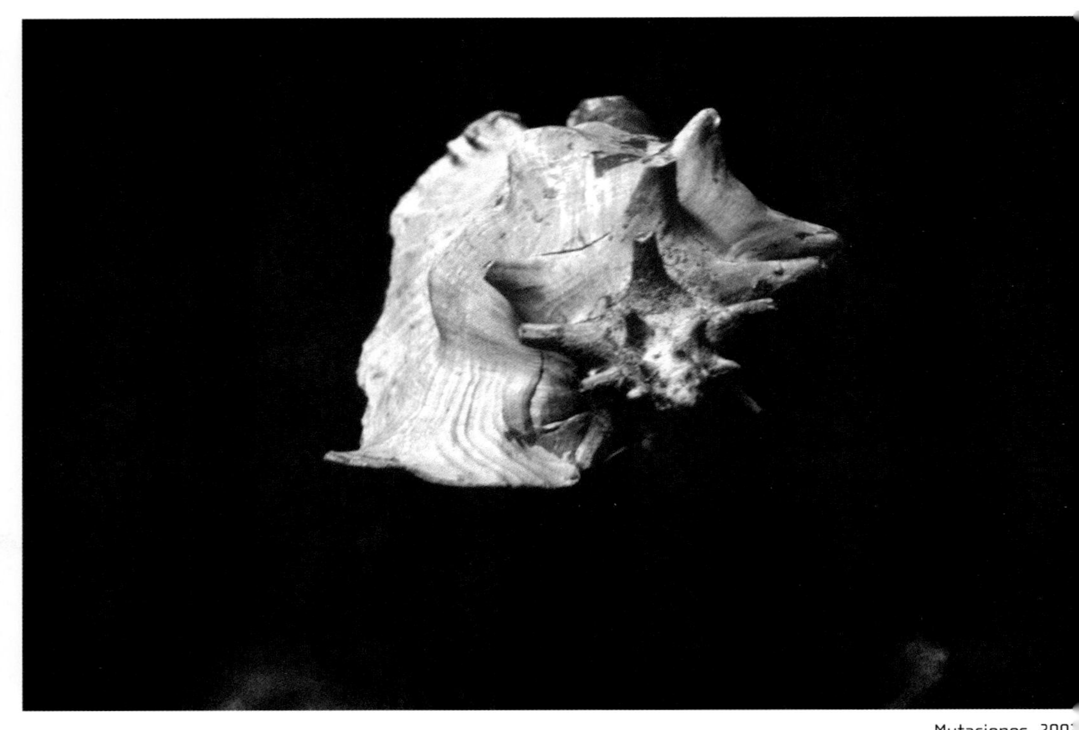

Mutaciones, 200

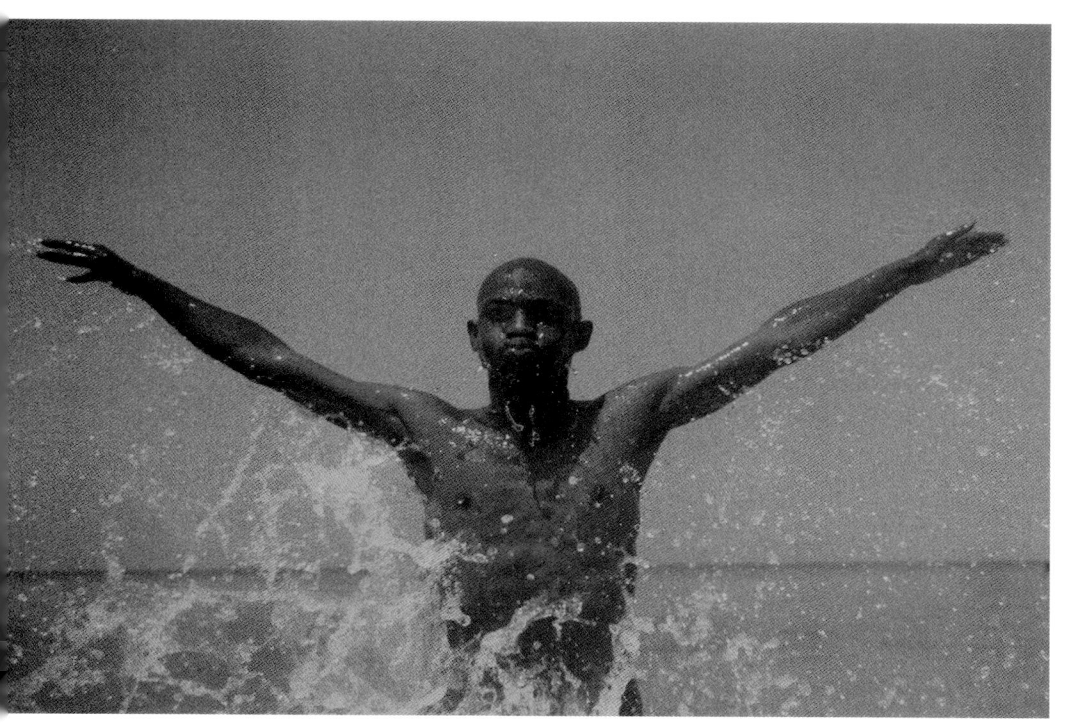

Sin título, 2003

Atibo-Legba, L´ouvri baye pou mwen, Agoe!
Papá-Legba, L´ouvri baye pou mwen
Pou mwen pase
Kile m a tune, m a salye lwa yo
Vaudou Legba, L´ouvri baye pou mwen
Pou mwen sa rantre
Kile m a tune m a remesyé lwa yo, Abobo!

Atibo-Legba, ábreme la barrera, Agoe!
Papá-Legba, ábreme la barrera
Para pasar yo cuando yo retorne, yo saludaré a los Loas
Vaudou Legba, ábreme la barrera
Para yo volver a entrar
Cuando yo retorne, agradeceré a los Loas, Abobo!

(Invocación a Legba—San Pedro para los católicos—
divinidad Vaudou que abre y cierra los caminos,
guardián de las encrucijadas, intérprete de los Loas)

From Me to We

Transforming Ourselves to
Greater Awareness

Joan Marques

Satinder Dhiman

Richard King

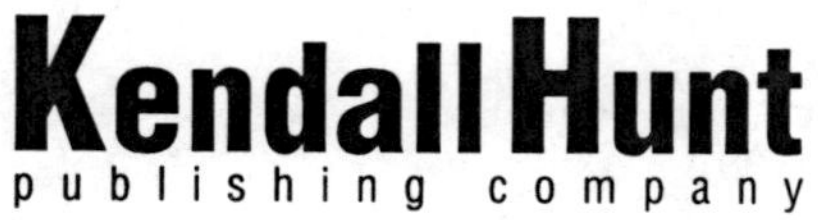

Kendall Hunt publishing company

Contents

From the Authors

It is with great pleasure that we present you this book of lessons for work and life, inspired by a series of gatherings among current and future members of the corporate and non-profit workplace in Los Angeles. The chapters in this book were carefully selected from conferences and dialogue sessions, held between 2006 and 2010.

Due to the rich backgrounds of the contributors, we have ensured deep insights and useful reflections, presented in a wide variety of ways. Some chapters are focused on topics that are critical in today's workplaces, such as workplace spirituality, character, inner- and inter-connection, and mindfulness, while others are more of a reflective nature, entailing life stories that cause us to contemplate and rethink our actions.

The chapters are written by three authors, Joan Marques, Satinder Dhiman, and Richard King. However, many chapters are inspired by presentations by other business executives. To ensure proper credit is given to those individuals, there are bios of the original topic presenter(s) included after each chapter. It should be stressed that, while inspired by several speakers, the chapters entail the interpretations of the authors of this book on the speakers' presentations.

The last chapter is the longest, as it entails business advices from people who have earned their credits in various performance fields. Some pieces of advice are very concise, while others are very elaborate. Yet, all have one thing in common: they are strong, from the heart, and very useful for those who feel inspired to make a positive difference in the world.

We wish you much reading and learning pleasure!

Dr. Joan Marques, Dr. Satinder Dhiman, & Dr. Richard King

Chapter I

Transform Your Workplace: Do Well By Doing Good

Abstract

The need for greater awareness is increasing as we get confronted with appalling and harmful behaviors of major corporations in our times. This chapter presents some powerful thoughts from business leaders and management scholars, presented at a 2007 conference in Los Angeles with the theme "Transform Your Workplace: Do Well By Doing Good." Statements will be presented from Dr. Christa Metzger, Mr. Bill Herren, Mr. Gary Hickman, Mr. Yoshito Yamaguchi, Dr. Joan Marques, Dr. Satinder Dhiman, and Dr. Richard King. In the final section of this chapter, the findings of a survey held after this conference will be shared.

Introduction

Even before the new millennium started, the speed of change and the degree of unpredictability in the world of work was a topic of major concern. As this era started, we were confronted with shocking events such as 9/11 and increasing examples and evidence of unethical behavior in business. As a result of this behavior, the workforce became more and more dissatisfied and fearful, and it became clear that initiatives needed to be taken to develop solutions. And where else could that happen but within ourselves, by following Gandhi's wise advice to "be the change we want to see in the world"?

In January 2007, the Business Renaissance Institute, in collaboration with the World Business Academy, organized an awareness conference with the theme *"Transform Your Workplace: Do Well By Doing Good."* The participants in this conference varied from corporate employees, academicians, and students to artists, philanthropists, and executives and owners of small, midsize, and large businesses.

The program was arranged in such a way that various aspects of spiritual behavior in work settings would be highlighted. This chapter provides a concise overview of the various presentations in this conference and the post-conference comments from participants.

Doing Well By Doing Good: Balancing Leadership and Personal Growth

Dr. Christa Metzger, professor in the Department of Educational Leadership and Policy Studies at California State University Northridge, reviewed an important issue within the "doing well" perspective: the personal aspect. Dr. Metzger provided interesting results from various studies, which she executed amongst school district superintendents, administrators, and school principals. The findings of these studies could easily be generalized to all workplaces, as they denote familiar problems for working people, and recurring reasons why workers get stressed and burned out. The main problem that many working people struggle with, according to Dr. Metzger, is finding a balance between one's personal and professional goals, and therefore, between one's personal and professional life. Dr. Metzger stressed that personal growth is key to the attainment of gratification and the prevention of enduring stress. She presented the following suggestions in this regard:

1. Taking care of yourself as well as you do others
2. Defining and applying your own themes of personal growth
3. Nourishing your spirit, finding time for solitude and meditation, and cultivating relationships
4. Fulfilling your purpose as a leader and finding meaning as a person

In light of the theme "doing well by doing good," Dr. Metzger found that, by learning to take care of yourself, you not only enhance your own work and life, but you also enhance the lives of people you encounter on a daily basis.

The Power of a Changed Life

Bill Herren, founder and CEO of American Vision Windows, shared a very touching story with the audience. It was the story of his own transformation from an athletic young man to an a homeless alcoholic, and subsequently from a man in search of meaning to a man who found meaning. Bill's story was moving, because it was filled with hope. It showed the audience that every transformation starts with the *will* to transform. Bill told the comical story of a goose pecking on his head during one of his days as a homeless man sleeping in the park. Although being chased by a wild goose was not as funny then to Bill as it is now, he admits that it became the turning point in his life. It forced him to rethink his life, wonder if that was what he wanted until the end of his days, and inspired him to change. He realized that he had been on a steady downslide through halfway houses, 12-step programs, Salvation Army visits, and other such programs, and that he needed to do something radical to clean up his act. Bill's turnaround came through a Bible that someone gave to him. As he started reading this book, he also started attending church. He started meeting different kinds of people: constructive, motivating, well-intending ones. This is also how he met his wife, Kathleen, a nice young lady, who inspired Bill even further to release his gloomy lifestyle and work himself up again on the ladder of life. From then on, life went uphill. Bill and Kathleen got married, and once their little family started expanding, they decided to buy a house. This is when they encountered a frustrating experience with a window delivery company, which led Bill and Kathleen to start their own window company: American Vision Windows. The rest is history. The organization grew into a multimillion dollar venture, but most of all, Bill's company continued to provide chances to those who had endured downfalls in life as he had.

Through his company, Bill now pays his blessings forward. American Vision Windows practices workplace spirituality in many ways: not necessarily because of its religious founders, but more because of the opportunities it provides to those with otherwise poor chances in today's high-demanding corporate world. Bill's company employs many ex-convicts, ex-homeless people, and ex-drug abusers. Bill is currently also involved in social projects in Lima, Peru. He vows, "My mission is to revolutionize the home improvement industry while changing the lives of our employees. I am going to make the industry answer the call."

In her epoch-making book, *Leadership and the New Science: Discovering Order in a Chaotic World*, Margaret Wheatley asks several profound questions. She wonders why so many organizations feel "dead" and seldom achieve expected results, why so many change efforts do not produce change and prove elusive. She further challenges us to find "elegant," "simpler" solutions to organizational problems and to create organizations that are "worthy of human habitation." She will certainly be delighted to read about American Vision Windows!

Passionate Participation

Gary Hickman, president of Junior Achievement (JA) of Southern California, presented a passionate speech, in which he explained the admirable task his organization fulfills toward upcoming generations of U.S. workers. One particularly fascinating story was about a young man who was heavily involved in gang activities, and had no belief in the world of legitimate work. Gary and his team felt compelled to change this young man's perspective, and they arranged several meetings with him. It soon became obvious that this young man, like so many youngsters these days, did not think that engaging in honorable work practices could get him anywhere. Yet, the JA team challenged him to think of something he would like to do, something in which he thought he could be successful. The young man came up with the idea of a maintenance company. The JA team initiated this project, and the young man's life got turned around positively. Today, he still runs his maintenance company, which was set up with the assistance and support of JA, and he serves as a great example to youngsters who are struggling with problems similar to those he had struggled with in his restless days.

Hickman's story underscored that having a purpose can make a great difference in a person's life. This story also reaffirmed Bill Herren's earlier point that transformation starts when the will to transform is ignited.

Are the Japanese Spiritual?

Yoshito Yamaguchi, senior managing director of Mitsubishi Electric Corporation and retired chairman of the board of trustees of Kwassui University in Nagasaki, Japan, brought in the inevitable and highly important international view. Mr. Yamaguchi, nicknamed "Super," presented an overview of spirituality in Japan from a cultural perspective. He emphasized the distinction between spirituality and religion, explaining that Japanese don't necessarily adhere to a specific religion, yet practice a highly spiritual mindset amongst one another. He discussed the lifelong employment habit within older Japanese corporations, as well as the changes that the Japanese culture has been undergoing in more recent years. He particularly reviewed the emergence of females in education and business participation, and concluded that Japanese are, indeed, very spiritual people.

Spiritual Performance From an Organizational Perspective

In a triangular presentation, the founders of the Business Renaissance Institute, Dr. Joan Marques, Dr. Satinder Dhiman, and Dr. Richard King, critiqued the performance of one or more well-known corporations, and defined what could determine the level of spirituality within these corporations.

Dr. Marques reviewed the Starbucks Corporation, and approached it from three angles:

1. Suppliers and societies
2. Employees
3. Customers

Her choice of Starbucks was based on the company's stellar ranking on various lists, such as those created by *Fortune, Business Ethics, Working Mother,* and the Great Places to Work Institute. Due to the fact that there were many MBA students in the audience, Marques also noted that Starbucks was also listed in the November 2006 edition of *Jungle,* the magazine for MBAs, as the No. 1 company that MBAs want to work for, because they consider it a company with "conscience." The criteria that the MBAs handled for companies with conscience were:

1. Leadership position
2. Financial health
3. Progressive working environment
4. Commitment to innovation
5. Corporate social responsibility

First focusing on suppliers and societies, Dr. Marques mentioned the term "enlightened self-interest," which Starbucks' previous president and CEO, Orin Smith, used when describing the corporation's relationships with stakeholders worldwide. Enlightened self-interest entails that, while the company is aware of its purpose of making profits, it strives to do so in such a way that the other party wins too, and preferably even more stakeholders than just the other party. Marques reviewed various sources in which Starbucks' approach of mutuality was displayed, starting with the story of Estuardo Porras, a Guatemalan coffee grower who managed to elevate the quality of life of all the plantation's employees and their families, and ending with an overview of the company's involvement in social and charitable practices in other parts of the world as well as in the United States.

Subsequently highlighting the corporation's approach toward employees, Marques referred to a wide variety of arrangements such as tuition reimbursement, partner benefits, wellness programs, and granting all employees who work more than 20 hours a week stock options and health-care benefits. She zoomed in on the touching story of a 1997 robbery at a Washington, DC, Starbucks store, during which three employees were murdered. Howard Schultz, at that time still president and CEO of the company, immediately chartered a plane and took charge: he visited the families, attended the funerals, decided that all future profits of this Starbucks would be allotted to organizations working for victims' rights and violence prevention, and later dedicated his book to these three fallen employees. With this and other stories, Marques illuminated the behavior of a leader who may not necessarily be labeled as spiritual, but who undoubtedly executes spiritual behavior.

Regarding Starbuck's dealings with customers, Marques highlighted the corporation's partnership with Magic Johnson's Los Angeles-based real estate development firm, Johnson Development Corp., through which 42 Starbucks stores were opened in ethnically diverse and underserved urban areas. Starbucks' care for customers is, according to Marques, also demonstrated in its recent decision to secure customers' health by eliminating from its menu milk that contains growth hormones.

Marques emphasized that the Starbucks Corporation clearly engages in spiritual performance, although it is not often referred to as such. This performance was ignited and encouraged by Howard Schultz, the man who purchased the company in the eighties and made it what it is today. Schultz's early life confrontations with insecurity and poor employment coverage (of his father) increased his compassion toward the positions of workers, and encouraged him to implement very humane arrangements for his employees today.

Marques' presentation could be captured in the following essential points:

- Organizations can make great profits while still behaving spiritually. "Enlightened self-interest" is an interesting principle of doing well while ensuring betterment for all stakeholders.
- Treating employees well and granting them more than the minimal provisions translates to enhancement of the corporation's own position in its industry.
- Serving underserved, oftentimes underestimated, markets pays off, not only in gratitude, but also in financial well-being and organizational expansion. Management strategist Gary Hamel refers to this phenomenon as "looking where no one else looks," and Tom Peters

calls it "doing the job no one else wants to do, and doing it well." Both of these gurus express the same message with their statements, though: value lies in areas that others undervalue.

• Spiritual behavior in organizations is rewarded most when exerted at macro as well as micro levels: globally and locally, externally and internally.

Dr. Satinder Dhiman explored the mega question:

Can humans run successful organizations humanely?

From an individual's point of view, this question boils down to the following: Is it possible to do work that is mind-enriching, heart-fulfilling, soul-satisfying, and financially rewarding? From an organizational standpoint, this question signifies running successful organizations humanely, with a high sense of service and social responsibility. Too often organizations get blindsided by their quest for profit maximization without paying any attention to human values and social costs. Dhiman's presentation explored some examples that provided an initial glimpse into the possibility of creating humane organizations. He began with Wal-Mart and Costco comparison to underscore the fact that it is possible to run two similar companies on different operating principles. Later on, he shared some interesting insights comparing IKEA with Home Depot.

There is no question that Wal-Mart's drive to offer "everyday low prices" has saved consumers billions of dollars. "But at what cost?" you may ask. As one analyst has observed: "You can find great bargains at Wal-Mart, but if you are a Wal-Mart employee, you may not be able to afford them." But there is a company challenging the Wal-Mart supremacy: Costco Wholesale Corp. Costco is breaking the Wal-Mart mold by treating its employees like human beings, without indulging into the empty rhetoric of calling its employees "associates." The formula, as it turns out, is very simple: treat your employees well, and they will treat your customers well. In a recent *New York Times* article, one marketing analyst complained that at Costco, "It's better to be an employee or a customer than a shareholder." Consequently, the Costco phenomenon represents a shift from treating your *shareholders* well to treating all of your *stakeholders* well.

How has Costco been able to avert most of the sins of modern capitalism? One does not need a PhD in labor economics to figure that out. Costco CEO Jim Senegal explains: "We pay much better than Wal-Mart. That's not altruism. It's good business." Good wages and benefits are why Costco has extremely low rates of turnover and theft by employees, he said.

And happier, well-compensated workers are more productive and loyal. Consequently, Costco enjoys one of the lowest turnover rates in the retail industry. Imagine the plight of Wal-Mart, which has one of the highest rates of employee turnover, in terms of recruiting, testing, and training new hires.

When you take a good care of your employees, so goes the logic, they are willing to get the job done and to do whatever it takes to make the company look good. Here is a story recounted by James O'Toole that underscores the point:

> In Southern California, a crazed motorist recently attempted to commit suicide by driving his car onto railroad tracks. At the last moment, he thought the better of it, abandoned the car, and ran home. Unfortunately, seconds later a full commuter train crashed into the car, leading to terrible loss of life and to severe injuries to hundreds of people. The accident occurred directly in the back of a Costco Warehouse store. Almost immediately, the blue-collar Costco employees organized themselves into an emergency brigade, and, armed with forklift trucks and fire extinguishers, set out to rescue trapped passengers, and to deliver first-aid to the wounded.

The corporate scandals perpetuated by companies such as Enron, WorldCom, and Tyco have heightened the public awareness regarding an organization's ultimate obligation to community. The civic elections of March 2002 in the Bay Area, CA, illustrate this point very well. Focusing on the residential impact of the proposed opening of IKEA in Palo Alto and Home Depot in Mountain View, the voters voted down Home Depot measure by two to one for being a poor neighbor. IKEA won with a narrow margin.

Dhiman concluded his part of the presentation by summarizing the following *principles of running successful organizations humanely:*

1. You can run a successful company based on the principles of servanthood.
2. Servanthood here refers to serving your customers and changing the lives of your employees.
3. When you take good care of your employees, they will take good care of your customers.
4. Satisfied, well engaged, and passionate employees are productive employees.
5. The passion level of employees runs very high when they believe that they are serving a higher purpose.

6. At the end of the day, ask what it is that we are not doing for our employees and what it is that we are not doing for our customers.
7. You can build a company on Godly principles and achieve success in the secular world. You can do well by doing good.

Dr. Richard King emphasized the "bottom line" impact of spirituality in the workplace and emphasized that workers at all levels want to feel that they represent more than a mere tool of organizational profit. People want meaning in their work, people want to contribute and be more productive and want to work in an environment where they don't have to check their values at the workplace door. They want a sense of "oneness."

Something is stirring in people's souls for a more humane work environment, increased simplicity, more meaning, and a connection to something higher. Too many people feel unappreciated, insecure, unhappy, and unfulfilled in their jobs.

King shared with the audience the research that he and his colleagues conducted by asking employees to answer the question, "How can I establish a more satisfying workplace for me and my colleagues?" The responses include:

- By continuing to think of the positive and good things about all of the people in my environment and of the environment itself.
- By starting each day with an optimistic attitude and leaving room for human error, disappointment, and change; keeping in mind that in order to grow and improve we must continue to learn each day.
- By listening to suggestions given by colleagues, because they might know something that we do not, and can possibly fix a problem our company might be having.
- By maintaining a positive attitude toward others, as well as ourselves, because we should realize that our attitude affects those around us.
- By treating others with respect and leaving as much negativity as possible out of the workplace (including negative aspects of our personal life).

King then gave an in-depth analysis of Southwest Airlines as a company that equates spirituality with productivity and profitability in the following manner:

- They seem to have a genuine sense of spirit and affection in both employees and customers.
- They have a strong emphasis in community, teamwork, serving others, employee connectedness, and customer care.

- They are consistently named to the list of 100 best companies to work for in the United States, as well as one of the top companies in corporate and social responsibility.
- They have high employee satisfaction and have one of the lowest turnover rates in the airline industry (6%).
- Even though SWA puts a strong emphasis on customers, it points out that its employees always come first. SWA seems to function like a big family.

Dr. King concluded the conference by sharing this Native American prayer:

> *Do all the good you can,*
> *In all the ways you can,*
> *With all the means you can,*
> *To all the people you can,*
> *As long as you can*

Survey Findings: Participants' Reviews

As a result of a post-conference survey among participants, it became clear that there is a need for this type of gathering on a regular basis. Members of today's workforce are searching for examples and impulses that can aid them in determining their own work-life balance. It was the general opinion of participants that the conference provided an excellent learning experience, was well organized, and presented thoughtful topics. Several attendees responded that they felt encouraged by the idea that, through the speeches, it had become more clear to them that it is really possible to do well while doing good in workplaces. Participants also complimented the strong time management maintained, which kept the interest level high throughout the conference. The feedback suggested creating room for even more participation from attendees, which will be incorporated in future conferences. Participants further seemed to agree that many spiritual corporations are not very tall, but for that matter more closely connected with their workforce and other stakeholders. In line with the above, participants encouraged the conference organizers to consider more targeted information on how to implement some of the spirituality-based ideas on a practical basis.

Dr. Joan Marques has more than 20 years' experience in advertising, radio and television production, show-hosting, and dynamic entrepreneurship, in both Suriname, South America, and Burbank, CA. She founded and managed a business and a non-profit organization prior to her immigration to the United States. Dr. Marques holds a BS in business economics from MOC (Suriname), an MBA from Woodbury University, and a doctorate in organizational leadership from Pepperdine University. She has done significant research on the topic of "spirituality in the workplace," and has authored multiple chapters and eight books, pertaining to workplace contentment, emotional intelligence, and leadership, for audiences in different continents on the globe. Her current research interests include workplace spirituality and awakened leadership.

Dr. Satinder Dhiman has guided business leaders for the last 25 years, and served for 10 years as a senior lecturer in commerce at DAV College in North India. He has co-authored various textbooks in the area of accounting and management, and currently serves as professor and chair of management as well as associate dean of business in Woodbury University's graduate program. Dr. Dhiman is the recipient of the 2004 ACBSP International Teacher of the Year Award and 2006 Steve Allen Excellence in Education Award. His research interests include transformational leadership, spirituality in the workplace, and mindfulness in life and leadership. Dr. Dhiman is the co-editor of *Spirituality in the Workplace: What it Means; Why it Matters; How to Make it Work for You* (Personhood Press, 2008) and the co-author of *The Workplace and Spirituality: New Perspectives in Research and Practice* (Skylight Paths, 2009). He holds a doctorate in organizational leadership from Pepperdine University and has completed advanced executive leadership programs at Harvard, Wharton, and Stanford.

Dr. Richard King is a recognized authority on United States-Pacific Rim business relations, and founded his company, King International Group, to carry out his personal commitment to strengthening these relations. He has held top management positions at major organizations and currently serves on the boards of various Pacific Rim-oriented organizations. He is a longtime member of the Noetic Institute and the World Business Academy. Dr. King is a frequent writer and speaker on Pacific Rim business issues, and is the initiator of the Business Renaissance consulting project, which focuses on "adding humanity to the bottom line." He holds a BS from Syracuse University, an MA from Occidental College, and an honorary doctorate of business administration from Woodbury University.

Chapter II

A Call for Personal and Professional Awareness

Abstract

The best way to instigate change is to start with ourselves. In June 2007 a dialogue session was held at the Caltech Athenaeum in Pasadena. A diverse blend of 41 Los Angeles–based business executives gathered together to dialogue about the essence of work and life. The purpose of the gathering was to share insights about personal and professional transformation. Three panel members were identified to initiate the process of sharing, and a rich contribution from the other attendees followed. Awareness of self and the immediate and larger environment formed the foundation of the verbal exchange of the evening.

Introduction

When a dialogue session for businesspeople in Los Angeles is organized, there is one fact guaranteed: diversity. Diversity is always an asset, but when people need to brainstorm about anything, it grows from being an asset to becoming an absolute wealth. This was also obvious during the dialogue night, organized by the Business Renaissance Institute in June 2007 at the Caltech Athenaeum in Pasadena. Business executives from many industries, large, mid-size or small, old and young, and from multiple cultural backgrounds, gathered together to dialogue about the essence of work and life. The purpose of the evening, which was to obtain more clarity about personal and professional transformation, gave rise to an atmosphere of interconnectedness and human awareness.

Panel Dialogue and Findings

In order to ensure proper interaction and the input of multiple perspectives, three panel members from entirely different industries were identified from among the attendees: one from the non-profit world, one from the for-profit environment, and one from academia. These panel members briefly reviewed their careers, elaborated on the changes that occurred from their personal and professional perspectives, and explained their current beliefs regarding career and purpose in life; they ended with a personal message to the group.

Even though they represented entirely different backgrounds and industries, all three panel members concluded that they found much more gratification in the sense of contributing to the quality of life, not just for themselves, but also for those they were dealing with. The most significant element in their diversity was that the panel consisted of representatives of three generations: a member of the Silent Generation, a Baby Boomer, and a Generation X-er. The panel members shared with the audience that they had all, at some point in their career, been struggling with the question of the direction of their lives. However, they had all became aware that their daily practices should be gratifying and representative of a significant contribution to the well-being of society.

The Baby Boomer panel member, who had enjoyed a wealthy career in the stock market before finding his "true north," brought up an interesting statement. He commented that almost every activity could serve to the advancement of humanity, or its demise. It is in the hands of those who are involved in those practices to use their most positive and responsible insights in guiding their activities toward advancement rather than destruction.

The panel member who represented Generation X openly shared her daily self-reflection exercises, which entail a continuous quest for meaning. She talked about her human imbalances, caused by the continuous transformation she experienced. She also explained that the transformation process caused her to question her motives and objectives regularly.

The senior member of the panel, the Silent Generation representative, presented some enlightened insights gathered through a life of repeated mistakes, directional change, and search for fulfillment.

Some interesting conclusions drawn by the panel members at this dialogue night were:

1. Money should not be the sole driving motive behind one's daily tasks. It is far more important to engage in activities that provide personal and societal gratification, with financial rewards ultimately arriving as a logical consequence.
2. Internal change is happening continuously, due to the transformations we witness and experience around us. It is therefore important to

continue seeking one's true calling, and review how this calling benefits society as well.

3. Time is an important factor—more so today than ever before—so remaining active is a necessity. The world will not improve if we wait on others to do it.

Group Contributions

In the group session after the panel dialogue, many of the business executives shared their personal messages as well. Some interesting messages were:

- Everything is now part of our personal circle of concern. It's important to realize that. We cannot rely on others to resolve the problems of the world. We need to do it ourselves, and embed this realization in all our actions—all the time.
- It is in the hands of the current working generation to establish the work and living environment for future generations. Our behavior will be honed by the upcoming ones: If we do bad, they will do worse. If we do well, they will do better.
- Overcoming fear is the most important asset when you're trying to make progress. We can no longer settle in our current circumstances, because they are about to change. Once the concept and the advantage of change are ingrained in your system, your life will be much more rewarding.

Chapter III

Meaning on Monday Morning: How Can We Contribute to That?

Abstract

Who likes Monday mornings? If you ask this question of working people, chances are that very few will raise their hands. And yet, we can also wonder if this is how it should be, and if we cannot do anything about it. Inspired by the increasing interest in the topic of bringing and nurturing the spiritual mindset in workplaces, a second dialogue session was held at the Caltech Athenaeum in Pasadena in October 2007. For this occasion, a group of about 40 members of the corporate, entrepreneurial, and academic world congregated to dialogue about enhancing the meaning of work. The topic was "Meaning on Monday Morning," based on the notion that many working people seem to dread Monday mornings most of all in their work lives. The three initiators of this event first shared their thoughts about the meaning of connectedness and the creation of Meaning on Monday Morning from both employee and management perspectives. A panel consisting of three executives continued the session with reflections on motivating co-workers and points to ponder, and the audience contributed some valuable experiential exchanges to complete the session.

Introduction

Meaning on Monday Morning: three M's that don't seem to make much sense to the majority of working people. Monday mornings are generally considered dreadful, because they emphasize the end of a weekend in which family and friends stood at the center. Monday mornings conjure up images of impatient people, trying to wake up on their way to work, and grouchy toward everyone they meet on their path.

In a dialogue session of businesspeople from various industries, held at the Caltech Athenaeum in Pasadena, the Monday Morning problem was addressed: How could this dreadful time of the week be transformed into something meaningful? In order to formulate this answer some thought-provoking insights on the topic were shared by the initiators, a three-member panel, and a highly reflective audience.

The Meaning of Connectedness

Bertrand Russell, one of Britain's most famous philosophers, attended a birthday party when he was 95. At this occasion he was asked if he would die for his beliefs, upon which Mr. Russell answered, "No, because I could be wrong." With this statement, Russell indicated his beginner's mind, even at such a progressed age and with a respectable number of 110 books to his name. Russell displayed, through these simple words, that he still maintained a "don't know" mind, free from being hung up on wanting to be right.

The great Greek philosopher Aristotle posted in his book "Ethics" the following question: "What is the purpose of life?" Today, we ask this question differently: "If we need to live a purposeful and meaningful life, what are purpose and meaning then all about?" This is a means of coursing straight to the roots of spirituality. Spirituality ultimately asks the fundamental questions, "Why am I here? What is the purpose of life? And what it the purpose of my life in particular?"

There is an interesting story related to this theme. It dates back to pre-revolution Russia. A soldier stopped a rabbi at gunpoint and asked him, "Who are you, and what are you doing here?" The rabbi asked the soldier how much he was paid for asking these questions. When the soldier said, "19 kopecks," the rabbi replied that he would pay the soldier 20 kopecks if he wanted to stop him everyday and ask him the same questions. This is to illustrate the importance of being confronted with such fundamental questions on a regular basis, in order to enhance conscious living.

Aristotle approached the same fundamental question in a triangular manner. He stated that, if we look for a meaningful life, there are three ways to do so:

1. Living a pleasant life, which is devoted to the gratification of senses and materialistic perspectives. This, according to Aristotle, is a self-defeating proposition that does not deliver durable enjoyment.

2. Living a good life, in which one should discover and polish one's signature strengths. Signature strengths are the specific innate qualities or gifts every individual has.
3. Living a meaningful life, whereby Aristotle emphasized that personal meaning can only be achieved by relating one's signature strengths to the meaning and well-being of others. It is Aristotle's opinion that we can only find meaning in our life if we relate it to the rest of the world. This very much indicates the principle and importance of interconnectedness.

Relating to interconnectedness, there is a story of a sand doll that was in search of the meaning of life. One day, the sand doll came upon an ocean and wondered what this immensity before her entailed. She asked the ocean, "Who are you?" and the ocean said, "In order to find that out you have to step in." The sand doll carefully placed one foot in the ocean, and her foot immediately dissolved. The sand doll was a bit puzzled and distressed by this occurrence and asked the ocean why this had happened. The ocean answered, "You gave a part of yourself to understand me. If you want to understand me completely, you have to walk in altogether now." The sand doll walked in and became part of the ocean.

The beauty of this story is that we cannot find meaning standing on the side. We have to dive in, in order to find out what life has to offer.

The MMM Taxonomy

Achieving Meaning on Monday Morning starts with ourselves. It is important to create meaning for ourselves and others at work, definitely if we consider the following facts, which are only three examples of the emotions people have dealt with in recent years:

1. A March 2007 *Fox News* report concluded from a survey of 5,000 U.S. households that more than half of all respondents disliked their current jobs, compared to less than 40 percent in a similar survey conducted 20 years ago.
2. *The Knight Ridder Tribune Business News* reported in June 2006 that more than 23 million Americans are flat-out unhappy at work and aren't afraid to show it by undermining co-workers who actually care about their jobs.
3. According to PR-Web, "A new national survey has found that only 28% of U.S. workers at large companies (those with 1001+ employees)

are strongly satisfied with their job." This, of course, indicates that at least 72% are unhappy or less satisfied.

These and other survey findings at national and international levels, all indicating the decreasing levels of satisfaction among members of the workforce, should encourage us to consider what it is that we can do about this problem. Meaning is becoming increasingly important as people start to understand that there should be more to work than just a paycheck.

In various studies and interviews we conducted in the past years we found the following three levels involved in finding meaning:

1. Connection with yourself
2. Connection with others
3. A resulting mutuality that leads to greater performance

Resulting from these basics, we developed the MMM (Meaning on Monday Morning) Taxonomy, which indicates an inside-out approach toward improved quality of life at work.

As mentioned in the introduction to this chapter, Meaning on *Monday Morning* may appeal most to workforce members, because Mondays are considered the hardest at work. So, if we can establish a meaningful atmosphere on Monday morning, much of the success and gratification of the workweek is ensured.

If we use the above three layers—connection with self, connection with others, and the resulting mutuality—as a guide, we can present the following suggestions:

Connection With the Self

You should first turn inward in order to define for yourself what you consider meaningful. Subsequently, you need to formulate the qualities you harbor to create a meaningful atmosphere around you. A dual question to consider in this regard is:

1. Do you enjoy what you are currently doing? If not, you should start working on a change of direction toward a more meaningful work life.
2. What personal qualities do you have that can help increase meaning for yourself and others involved? By asking yourself this question, you start involving others in the picture. Based on your background, education, interest areas, religion, and other values, you will be able to

come up with a package of actions you can undertake to improve the atmosphere at work for yourself and other stakeholders.

Connection with Others

After determining the personal qualities you can use to contribute to improving the quality of life at your work, you can start reaching out. There are many simple actions you could consider, such as engaging in the art of immaterial giving by granting a smile, showing some genuine interest into the well-being of others, or making a genuine compliment. Empathy and understanding go a long way.

An important hint: finding a few colleagues who want to join in these affirmative activities may significantly enhance the success rate of creating a culture of mutuality in one's department.

Mutuality Toward Greater Performance

If you have succeeded in creating a more pleasant environment in your department, the following multi-layered results are likely to occur:

1. The atmosphere in the department will be less formal. There will be more cooperation and mutual support and, therefore, higher performance.
2. Other departments will hear about it. They may spontaneously adopt this culture, or you and your colleagues may take on the challenge to spread it.

Meaning on Monday Morning is good for you, your colleagues, customers and other stakeholders, and for business as a whole. When people have a better connection with each other, they enjoy being where they are, and they become more willing to perform as a team, to cover for one another, to ensure a prolonged existence of their department, and ultimately their organization. They will be more willing to seek solutions in downtimes, because they want to celebrate good times together. This is what ultimately enables any organization to excel beyond its competitors.

MMM From a Management Perspective

In the next section we will review what managers can do to create a happier, more harmonious, and more productive workplace. The first thing managers have to recognize is the importance of enhancing the quality of life as a whole rather than making decisions based solely on the bottom line. This process should be emanated through our employees. Today's managers should focus more on developing relationships and facilitating people rather than merely producing a quantifiable product or service. We should all make a serious effort to see ourselves as servant leaders, who are there to support their people.

Motivating employees does not only make employees feel better about themselves, but elevates their productivity and profitability also. Therefore, managers should motivate their employees and ensure their gratification. They should understand the importance of family and try to allow employees to maintain a balance between work and family. Managers should also develop a passion for their work, ensuring that they love what they do. When your heart is in your work, employees will know it, and you'll soon find that they've put their hearts in their work, too.

We should maintain high expectations for ourselves as well as for our co-workers. We have to keep our priorities in order: be tough and firm when needed, but also flexible, emphasizing the positive while de-emphasizing the negative. It's all about creating a positive environment. Therefore, we have to stay away from toxic situations and do whatever we can to create a happy, harmonious environment. As an extension to that, we have to treat our employees with respect and dignity; if we do, we'll receive the same in return. We have to give our employees recognition and show appreciation for what they do. Simple things mean a lot. Just thanking an employee for staying 30 minutes overtime can do so much more than all the formal material rewards would.

Communication, openness, transparency, informing employees about developments ,and refraining from keeping them in the dark are all significant steps toward improving the atmosphere at work. Our employees are our most important stakeholders, and they deserve to know what is going on. If a change is pending, let them in on it. Have them participate in the change. Get their thoughts about how to better handle this change. These are some of the things that managers can do to create a workplace with more meaning for Monday, Tuesday, Wednesday, Thursday, and Friday morning!

As managers, we don't send a memorandum out to state that we are going to be into spirituality. It has to be radiated through our behavior. Therefore, it takes a lot of work and energy. A spiritual workplace does not happen by circumstance. We also have to remember that if we send positive thoughts into the environment, it strengthens us, and if we send negative thoughts, it weakens us. We should lend a helping hand when we can. We further need to remind our employees that the most important thing at work is not their last or next raise, or their upcoming bonus; it is something unquantifiable: a non-materialistic substance. These are the kinds of things we should remind our employees and ourselves of.

The following two real life examples may illustrate the enactment of Meaning on Monday Morning.

1. A few decades ago one of the authors of this chapter was CEO of the Birtcher Corporation, a public corporation in medical electronics, and he was facing the challenging task of turning the company around. He invited the six vice-presidents who were in the organization at the time into one-on-one meetings, and asked each of them a series of three questions: The first question was, "Are you happy at this company?" Each of the vice presidents said that he was not. The second question was, "Why aren't you happy?" They answered that they felt underutilized and unappreciated and were unsure how they could really contribute to the company. The third question was, "How do you think you can contribute to the company?" Upon the answer to the third question, the CEO stated, "Well, then that's your job." The organization charts were destroyed and the mental boxes in which each of them were confined were torn up. Within two and a half years the company was turned around, the productivity and profitability were high, the savings were up, and about a year later the company could be sold to Hewlett Packard. The company was turned around by chaining life-purpose to work-purpose. There was no difference between the two, because, as human beings, we are only one person with one set of core values.

2. While working for the Kaiser Company, one of our associates was placed in charge of a 10 million dollar project. Unfortunately, the project failed. When Mr. Kaiser called our associate into his office after hearing about the project failure, this young man was expecting nothing else than to be fired. Yet, Kaiser did exactly the opposite: he invested an additional 10 million dollars in the young employee and offered him the option to work together in establishing a solid return on investment for this new project. The young associate of those days, now a seasoned business executive, stated that this was a great experience for him as a young man, and a tremendous motivator to become a star performer for this organization. Mr. Kaiser taught him this unforgettable lesson at that time: "Reward excellent failure, and punish mediocrity."

The above two examples provided good examples of how to provide meaning in the workplace. People want meaning and a sense of one-ness in what they do.

A good illustrative story in this regard is "The Way of the Goose,"[1] a story written by Robert McNeish:

> *This fall when you see geese heading south for the winter... flying along in V formation...you might consider what science has discovered as to why they fly that way:*
>
> *As each bird flaps its wings, it creates an uplift for the bird immediately following. By flying in V formation the whole flock adds at least 71% greater flying range, than if each bird flew on its own.*
>
> *People who share a common direction and sense of community can also make their journey easier if they are traveling on the thrust of one another.*
>
> *When a goose falls out of formation, it immediately feels the drag and resistance of trying to go it alone... and quickly gets back into the formation to take advantage of the lifting power of the bird in front.*
>
> *So, we learn from the goose that our way is easier if we join in formation with those who are headed in the same direction as we are.*
>
> *When the head goose gets tired it rotates back in the wing and another goose flies point. It makes sense, then, to take turns, whether you are men and women engaged in a common task or journey, or geese flying south.*
>
> *Geese honk from behind to encourage those up front to keep up their speed.*
>
> *Finally...and this is important...when a goose gets sick or is wounded by gunshots, and falls out of formation, two other geese fall out with him and follow him down to lend help and protection. They stay with the fallen goose until it is able to fly or until it dies, and only then do they launch out on their own, or join another formation to catch up with their group.*
>
> *If we have the sense of a goose, we will stand by each other like that.*

Panel Highlights

A diverse panel, consisting of members from different types of work environments, shared the following thoughts about Meaning on Monday Morning:

- From a day-to-day perspective it is important to make sure that managers at all levels communicate at the beginning of the week to lay the foundations for the other days.
- From a strategic angle, we need to consider the purpose of motivational activities that have to start at the hiring process of new employees and be implemented all through the performance of the organization, regardless of the industry it operates in.
- From a multicultural angle, we need to keep in mind that the implementation of Meaning on Monday Morning will vary from environment to environment, specifically when considering the divergence in cultures in various countries. In a collectivist society, a different approach will be appreciated compared to an individualist society, and so too in a masculine as opposed to a feminine community. When implementing Meaning on Monday Morning, managers should first understand what it is that the people in their environment need to feel satisfied and appreciated. This, then, should be given to them.

Examples from the Workplace About Creating Meaning

- Managers often make the mistake of piling on employees additional tasks that deviate from the initial reasons they were hired. These additional tasks may distract or even demoralize the employees and reduce their motivation and productivity at work. It is crucial for managers to regularly communicate with employees to find out whether their work still makes sense as it develops over time.
- Meaning is endorsed through human connection. The percentage of individuals with whom we can actually share real personal communication is decreasing in modern days. People are increasingly involved in viewing television, sitting behind their computers and surfing the Internet, and balancing the demands of a more demanding life pattern overall. Yet, it is crucial to give human beings some human attention now and then. A little bit of human attention can do what money and gifts cannot achieve. The following example may explain this:

In a highly diverse workplace, there was a young male worker who was going through spells of intense rage. All managers were concerned about this worker's behavior. One manager decided to make it a point to communicate with this young man on a daily basis, if only for five minutes sometimes. When things were extremely hectic, he would lend a hand lifting boxes or whatever needed to be done. Through this connection, the young man started changing. He felt recognized and appreciated, and his rage spells disappeared.

- From a multicultural perspective it is crucial for us to realize that we cannot merely assume that all workers in our workplace adhere to the same values. While the United States is a monochronic society when it comes to time management, many of the members of the U.S. workforce may adhere to polychronic mindsets. Understanding this difference, and allowing workers their space to be effective in their own way, may serve as a major means toward creating meaning in any workplace.

Final Statements

Openness toward others, increased tolerance, and understanding can make a world of difference in the way employees feel in their workplace. In an increasingly diversified world of work it is crucial for members of any workplace to realize that much more can be achieved when people decide to respect one another, and demonstrate willingness to communicate with and learn from each other.

The power of connectedness can be illustrated with this little testimony: A female business executive explained that, after 20 years of swimming in a prestigious corporate ocean where she did not feel happy, she shifted to a different environment where she earned far less than before, but felt infinitely happier. Her message, based on personal experience, was for all of us to first consider our match with our workplace and cease being driven only by financial rewards.

It is also important to realize that one organization might have entirely different subcultures, where you can have, for instance, one happy floor and one sad floor. Members of the workforce, regardless of their level or rank in the organization, should be aware of these differences and do something about the imbalance. This could happen top-down (initiated by management) or bottom-up (initiated by employees), or perhaps in multi-layered teams that take it upon themselves to improve the atmosphere in the workplace.

And then there is the discrepancy in perspectives between top management and workers at lower levels. It often happens that ground-level workers complain about top management's lack of outreach, while top management, from their side, complain about the obstinate attitude of lower-level workers. Many people are shocked when they find out how they are perceived by those who observe them only from a distance. In order to elicit improvement at work, members of the workforce at any level should examine their own humanity first, and scrutinize the way they are perceived by others. In this process they should not use their inner circle as a frame of reference, but rather approach members of groups that view them from a distance. This may serve as a valuable eye opener for all parties and enhance understanding as to how one is perceived by members from other groups.

Conclusion

This chapter presented a number of important points for workers at all levels to consider. There are valuable advises for workers at all levels enclosed. Top managers, middle managers, and floor workers alike can benefit from the perspectives shared in this chapter. Reflection outside of the comfort zone may be a great asset when people think they are already doing the right thing toward their co-workers. They may be surprised to find what others think about them. Sensitivity toward alternate cultures is also crucial in establishing a more meaningful work environment. In the ever-changing world of work today, we get confronted with many different cultures and mindsets. Maintaining an approach of tolerance can enhance the speed of gratification, effectiveness, and efficiency at work.

Meaning is an interconnected matter. It cannot merely exist for the self. It starts internally, but needs to be applied toward others to be effective and to create a sense of purpose. Establishing Meaning on Monday Morning can start with a small gesture toward colleagues, clients, and anyone else one encounters in the workplace, but it can have tremendous results that positively affect one's sense of self-worth as well as the organization's well-being.

Chapter IV

People, Products, and Planet

(based on a presentation from Dr. David Rosen at the Business Renaissance Institute on June 28, 2008)

While the call for environmental sustainability is mounting worldwide, corporations accelerate their efforts to retain markets by "going green." Yet in order for their returns on investments to be met, businesses are shifting from the production of goods alone to the production of values that will create a market for their goods. From the customer's side, there are challenges: what at first glance may seem "green" may not be. Whether and how much true sustainability can be achieved when business is producing "green goods," both as product and value, is an interesting point of contemplation.

About Habits and Choices

Sustainability grows out of a paradigm of commerce in which the exchange of goods is most transparently an exchange of values. People do not simply buy objects or services. They buy the values that the products represent and that fit with their lives. Consider, for example, low-income families: they oftentimes choose to buy premium-quality products in stores with their food stamps, for the simple reason that they want to mirror the more affluent in society. Whether anyone decides to consider this a curse or advantage of social behavior depends on their position on this tendency. Individuals who consider the possibilities these low-income customers could have if they purchased generic brands will probably shake their head and disapprove. However, corporations, who are also aware of this buying behavior, consider it an advantage and effectively play into it.

While all parties are trying to make the choices they consider most gratifying, we are confronted with a mounting call globally for "going green" and, with that, ensuring greater environmental sustainability and human quality of life. This pressure toward more health-related responsibility in production is, of course, also felt by major corporations, and they respond, not necessarily because they are that compassionate toward the environment, but because they realize that it's the trend of these times and the most effective way to retain their markets.

One of the interesting developments in recent years is "luxury green," where major corporations assemble environmentally responsible gimmicks in products that are not exactly nature friendly, but highly preferred by the buying public. So, while the purpose is not really served when expensive wares, such as SUVs, are equipped with "green" add-ons, the customer feels satisfied, because he or she is participating in the latest trend!

Through our buying behavior, we display who we are and what we believe in: it's a value proposition, not so much in the sense of financial value, but rather in regards to the value we consider important to us.

And yet it's easy enough to remain healthy and environmentally friendly without spending large amounts of money on that. It just requires a mindset of awareness about your own well-being and the well-being of others. Walking more and driving less, for instance, keeps a person healthy and in shape, reduces air pollution, and helps with saving money, especially now with sky-high fuel prices. If we perceive the continuously rising numbers at the gas stations as a motivation to start walking more and driving less, the current trend may be considered a blessing rather than a reason to get upset.

Reflections on Environmental Sustainability

In today's and future business, the powerful ones will be those that respond quickest to new trends. Power is increasingly determined by trans-disciplinarily rather than a narrow focus. If you wonder what this shift in power-relationships entails, look to the San Francisco-based company IDEO, which specializes in human factors, psychology, business, design, engineering, and manufacturing, and thereby provides full-service consulting for product innovation and design to a broad array of customers.

The countries that get green fastest will have the economic lead in the next decades.

Every new trend is expensive at first before prices start decreasing. The economically weakest will first suffer from the go-green trend, particularly on basis of what was explained in the first part of this chapter: poor people mirror the buying patterns of affluent ones and want to purchase high-end products with their meager means, and corporations respond to this behavior within the go-green trend with luxury items, because a large majority of buyers feel that they make a statement about their whereabouts with the level of luxuriousness that their possessions represent.

Several European countries are leading in the go-green trend; their awareness of sustainability is much greater than that of the United States. In this regard, it's interesting to observe the world as a whole: while sustainability is still a non-issue in countries such as China, it is a major issue in European countries such as the Netherlands. The interesting dialogue that emerged in this regard was one pertaining to Hofstede's masculine versus feminine societies. When reviewing societies through Hofstede's lens, "masculinity" should be seen as the trait which emphasizes ambition, acquisition of wealth, and differentiated gender roles; while "femininity" needs to be perceived as the trait which stresses caring and nurturing behaviors, equality of sexes, environmental awareness, and more fluid gender roles. The conscious question to be contemplated is, How can a clearly "masculine" country such as the United States be educated to become "feminine" in spending patterns and behavioral traits? Sustainability is a feminine trait, and the fact that we talk about "Mother Earth" and "Mother Nature" should be an indicator of that. It is crucial for all of us to get more in touch with our feminine side, even though it may not sound as attractive, initially, to the male nature.

Each one of us can engage in individual behavioral adjustments in order to help change the environment. As mentioned in this chapter, we can decide to walk more and drive less when we have to cover short distances. There are numerous ways in which we can make shifts in our lives toward overall improvement. Those of us who realize this option and execute it should encourage others to think about and implement positive personal changes as well.

In our attempts to ignite a positive awareness on spending patterns and consumer behavior, we should still be cautious, because people have grown accustomed to having a choice. The fact that the United States is still the most sought after country in the world for immigration indicates that it is very human to prefer a broad array of choices, which is exactly what the United States represents. On the other hand, it is wise to realize that even an affluent nation such as the United States needs to start thinking massively about its behavior. Without responsible sacrifices, we are heading straight for chaos. If people continue to drive uninhibitedly, despite of fuel prices going through the roof, an era of devastating poverty will await us. A society can also learn, and it might be useful for this society to learn how to ration, redefine its social measures, and correct its spending behavior.

One example of the positive trends in business is the establishment in North America of the Norwegian car corporation TH!NK, an initiative which was the result of a partnership with United States-based clean-tech investors. TH!NK manufactures electrical vehicles that have zero local emission and superior energy efficiency. The TH!NK *City,* one of the modern urban cars manufactured by this corporation, is 95% recyclable and made of recycled materials. The interesting story behind TH!NK is that this car was already introduced in the United States in the nineties without much success, because neither the manufacturing community nor the purchasing community was ready for a project of that nature. Another development is the awareness of bottled water. Increasing numbers of voices go up about the health hazard of plastic bottles. Several cities have already jumped on the "ban bottled water" bandwagon.

Conclusion

Changing a society's thought patterns, values, and general behavior will take time. Massive change is a slow process. Yet, it is not impossible if the realization exists that something needs to be done. Just as corporations are continuously benchmarking within—and now also outside of—their industries to learn from and adopt best practices, so too can countries. The United States can benchmark spending and environmental awareness initiatives from other (European) countries. At the personal level, we can benchmark responsible behavior from people we encounter at work or in other social settings. We can learn from those who refrain from allowing societal trends and general perspectives to determine their spending patterns and behavior in daily life. The choice to become environmentally responsible and more empathetic toward our fellow humans starts with our individual behavior.

People determine what *products* they want to use, and with that, they influence the well-being of the entire *planet.*

David Matthew Rosen is senior vice president at Woodbury University. He received a BA in English from Haverford College and a PhD in English from the Johns Hopkins University.

His publications include *The Changing Fictions of Masculinity*, published by University of Illinois Press, and "The Volcano and the Cathedral" in *Muscular Christianity: Embodying the Victorian Age*, published by Cambridge University Press.

Chapter V

Character and Leadership at Work

(based on a presentation from Dr. Joyce Millikan at the Business Renaissance Institute on August 16, 2008)

Our character is an important factor in how we perceive our lives and the things we experience. Character is crucial is relationships, whether at work, at home, or in other social environments. It is also our character that determines what type of leader we are. Important for succeeding in today's fast-paced world is adaptability to change. If we consider that our character is the driver of our behavior, we can easily understand how much it has to do with our level of preparedness as well. In this chapter we present some crucial insights on character for members of today's workforce at any level.

What Character Means

Character is something we all possess, but don't talk or think about as often as we should. Character is determined by various influencing factors around us: our parents, peers, social environment, and culture, to name just a few. In the United States, the dominant trait of individualism has presented us with numerous advantages, but with some indisputable disadvantages as well. Social isolation, for instance, is a growing problem in America these days. Several sources have found that too many people lack any contacts with whom they can communicate on a trusted level. While people do have colleagues with whom they socialize at work, real connections are lacking to a concerning degree. Interestingly, there seem to be different dimensions to inter-human connection as well. Did you know, for example, that there is a higher degree of racial intermingling than educational? This means that people from different ethnic backgrounds mix together more easily than those who may be of the same race, but represent different educational levels.

Character has everything to do with leadership. In this perspective, we define "good leadership" as the ability to motivate people to work together enthusiastically. This process of motivation happens through our inner strength to serve as models and inspire those who follow us. Good leaders lead by personal example. In other words, they walk their talk.

When we look deeper into the relationship between character and leadership, we can even transcend the level of merely being a "good" leader by becoming a spiritual leader. A spiritual leader is one who appreciates and seeks accountability, listens and understands others, learns and applies learning to his or her life; exceeds expectations of others and self; contributes generously, giving more than they thought they had; and offers spiritual guidance and assistance to others who want to succeed in life.

If we now review leadership in the scope of character, we find that our beliefs, values and standards; vision and sense of purpose; and perspectives on profit-sharing, communication, and accountability are crucial to our success in the workplace, as well as to the overall success of the organization. In today's world of work it becomes increasingly mainstream for companies to go the extra mile and accommodate their employees by sponsoring counseling sessions, offering deductibles in health insurance, and providing employee guidance.

It is the leader who sets the tone in the organization or department he or she leads and can significantly influence to what degree employees will assist and support one another. Consider Herman Miller, the well-known furniture company that believes in the talents of many and the uniqueness of each: this company has a great participative approach that gives employees a sense of ownership and serves as a great encouragement in their performance.

That being said, we do need to be cautious for corporations with highly spiritual mission and vision statements and leaders with heart-touching statements, because they don't always walk their talk. Think, for instance, about this statement: "One of the most satisfying things in life is to perform in a moral environment where people maintain values." This is a statement from the late Kenneth Lay, founder and chairman of Enron, once one of the world's leading electricity, natural gas, pulp and paper, and communications companies, and now a popular symbol of willful corporate fraud and corruption. This infamous example of beautiful but hollow words teaches us that we should focus not only on leaders' statements, but even more on their behavior. Do people live their talk? Character is important.

There is an interesting video clip of a janitor who was mopping the floor but failed to place the "Wet Floor" warning sign in the hallway. Unfortunately, a person entered the hallway, slipped, fell, and lost consciousness. The janitor, highly alarmed by what had happened, realized his failure, looked around, quickly got the warning sign out, placed it aside the unconscious person, and disappeared, hoping that no one had seen what happened. This clip illustrates that it is tempting to save our reputation and job, even if that means refraining from doing the right thing. In case of the janitor, he knew he might get in major trouble by admitting his mistake and seeking help for the person who slipped and fell, so he acted unethically by covering up his error after the damage was done, and leaving the victim where he was.

Character is an important factor in our lives. It can be described in many ways, and when we think of cases such as the one described above, character can be presented as *what you do when you think no one is looking.* Every decision we make ultimately impacts others. Character determines our responses. It builds our decisions. It helps us to do what is right. Character is the root system that supports our entire life. If we think of ourselves as a tree, our achievements are the visible fruits that result from the roots of the tree, our character.

Strong character thinks and sees past material advantage. It realizes that money can buy many things but not the gratification that one seeks in life. Character is responsible for the subtle but immensely important differences that make life worthwhile. It can change a house into a home, and provide satisfaction in a job. People of strong character ensure success in any organization. Character entails doing what is right because it is the right thing to do.

Can Character Change?

There are many organizations who pay much money for consultants to come in and organize workshops and seminars on ethical behavior and other character-related issues. While these workshops may be useful to many, there will always be people who refuse to change their behavior, keep themselves closed to any thought-provoking issue, and obstruct positive change. Leadership of organizations should therefore realize that character-based workshops will draw out and enhance excellence in those who have a positive will to succeed and do well, but will make those who already harbored a negative mindset even worse. It will then be up to top management of such an organization to take appropriate measures.

Another problem is hypocrisy, which is also a character problem. Should we simply assume that any CEO who invites character-shaping workshops in their organization is one who already masters good character? Not necessarily. Usually, the CEOs who invite these workshops in realize that there is always room for improvement, in everyone, including themselves. Leaders with weak characters usually don't invite such programs into their organizations. If they do, it usually means that they are ready to apply some thorough self-examination and change for the better.

Conclusion

Character is expressed in many ways, especially through the little things we may consider unimportant or invisible to others. A leader's character is determined not by his or her facilitation of workshops, seminars, or even mentoring to employees, but by the level of modesty and humility this leader combines with his or her determination, business acumen, and negotiation skills. Some leaders may, for instance, be concerned as to whether, when goals are achieved, their employees will realize that the leaders also played a part. Many teams have been led from chaos and disaster to success, and have ultimately failed to see what their leader has done for them, saying, "We have done it ourselves." The wisest thought to consider for a leader who gets confronted with this situation is that character exists in everyone. It does not only work top-down, but also bottom-up. Employees with strong characters will realize who helped them in their growth. Those who cannot see that the leader supported them in their advancement are of weak character, and not worth dwelling on. In today's work environment, the concept of "leader" increasingly transcends into "facilitator." When you do your job right, people will no longer need you, and that is when you have done a great job.

Joyce Millikan, PhD, is CEO and co-founder of Working Faith and principal at Character Works! A USC grad (1971), Joyce earned her MA (1994) and PhD (2003) from Fuller Theological Seminary in Pasadena, CA. Dr. Millikan serves privately held businesses, non-profit organizations, and public and private educational institutions to implement a character-based leadership model that brings lasting benefits to the bottom line, to clients, vendors, employees and families. Joyce and her husband, Greg, live in Pasadena. They enjoy regular rides together on a tandem recumbent bicycle, and enjoy grandparenting six grandchildren.

Chapter VI

Challenges of a Spiritual Journey: A Personal Reflection

(based on a presentation from Dr. Sanford Shapero at the Business Renaissance Institute on October 25, 2008)

If we reflect on our lives, we can learn many things from our experiences. The greatest teacher resides within. Unfortunately, it takes many years before we actually realize and accept that. But if we listen to or read about the life stories of others, we can also learn much through reflection. This chapter presents the reflections of a spiritual journey from an ordained rabbi who decided to focus on a greater good for a greater number. Dr. Sanford Shapero, former president of City of Hope, and founding director of Los Angeles Orthopedic Hospital's Center for Gerontology, presents some interesting reflections that are timeless and particularly useful for members of today's workforce at any level.

A Fascinating Journey

Every life represents a fascinating journey that can serve as a reflective lesson to those who follow in our footsteps. Looking back from this blessed state I have achieved in years, I can truly attest that my life has been an enriching and gratifying journey. In my younger years I practiced as a rabbi, but found that there were many influences around me that determined a different course than the one I had originally envisioned. People come and go in our lives. Some make deeper impressions on us than others. Teachers, parents, and friends— they are all among those who may shape our perspectives on life.

The Civil Rights Movement

One of the most influential individuals in my life was Dr. Martin Luther King, Jr., whose work I supported as a young rabbi, first through donations to the civil rights movement, and later through a highly visible personal presence in the movement. These were the turbulent, highly segregated and overly sensitive sixties, but young as I was, I was dedicated to stand for something I believed in. Along with 17 other rabbis, I decided to make witness to the movement, but our efforts were not appreciated, so we were promptly thrown in jail. It was particularly this experience that made me realize that, at that time, certain groups had no voice and no rights. It was also through this close involvement in the civil rights movement that I developed a strong sense of awareness for the needs of those in deprived situations.

Just like Martin Luther King, Jr., I had very high regard for Mahatma Gandhi, the legendary non-violence freedom advocate from India. I actually had the privilege of communicating by mail with Gandhi during his lifetime! In one of my letters to this great leader, I asked him how he gained the emotional and mental willpower to become the man he was. Gandhi replied to me that in his younger days he, too, like so many youngsters, loved and enjoyed the good life. Gandhi explained that he realized then that the only true need in life was hunger. So, he starved himself to overcome even this need, thus developing the strength to demonstrate the effectiveness of non-violent opposition and lead his country to independence.

Acting upon your deepest beliefs is a courageous move, which many don't follow up on. Martin Luther King, Jr., did, and he paid with his life for this heroic decision. And many of those who worked with him side by side can attest to the fact that he would not leave his people in the cold. He was there when they needed him. In my own religious community, I soon got into trouble for my unconcealed support of the civil rights movement. But when things seemed to be at their worst, there was Dr. King to talk to my superiors and advocate my actions in the eloquent way that he was so well-known for.

City of Hope

Some years later, I became the CEO at City of Hope, one of America's most prominent hospitals in cancer treatment and scientific research, and there I was confronted with a rich blend of organizational intrigues, arrogance, and senses of superiority among some of the highly educated staff members. Looking back today, I perceive this challenging time as an enriching lesson in advocating and successfully implementing diversity in my workforce. I learned to convince even the most abrasive corporate opponents to support the organization in difficult times, and realized that spirituality has a persona of its own. I experienced the power of a spiritual approach as if it were another entity, larger than myself, helping to shape my character. One major lesson I took with me from those years is to judge people not on external traits but on character. There was even a decisive moment when I forewent the hiring of a highly acclaimed, yet extremely haughty individual, and chose for the well-being of my team and the safeguarding of a spiritual approach instead.

One effort that I particularly pride myself on is the fact that I always kept the act of laying off my employees to a minimum. In dire financial times, I chose to communicate with my employees and creatively find solutions to keep the entire team intact. I did not pretend to know all the answers—because I didn't—but laid the problem before the group instead, and requested input from the members. Ultimately, no one was laid off, and the problems were resolved.

Wherever you work, you should always keep your ears and eyes open, so that you can continue learning, regardless of your position. I am thinking back, for example, to a time when assigned parking was instituted at my workplace. I soon learned that this was creating dissatisfaction among many workers. Many CEOs will create other sources of dissatisfaction to distract their workers from the initial reason. I decided to go the simple route: I simply refused to park in my assigned parking spot and started parking in general parking places. The assigned parking chapter was closed soon thereafter.

I served a total of 17 years at the City of Hope, 10 as the CEO. I learned, for instance, that it is important to establish a trustworthy governance group in order to nurture the spiritual mindset in your work environment. I therefore urge everyone who reads this to remain in touch with all your stakeholders, in whatever setting you may perform. Stakeholders form the lifeline of your organization.

Concluding Thoughts

Here are, in conclusion, some thoughts you may want to consider:

- Spirituality means purifying yourself from the corrupting influences of the world and dealing with your moral duty and obligations. Spirituality begins with you and how you set examples.

- Many organizations today are facing erosion of their ethical standards. Documents are altered, financial statements are fluffed up, and stakeholders are deceived. Yet, where top management leads with integrity, it re-emphasizes spirituality to employees and re-establishes trust.
- We are all servants to whatever we believe in. Let us make sure the cause of our belief is an honorable one.
- Keep thinking outside the box. If you fail between envisioning and acting, you're a manager, not a leader.
- Never stay in a situation that you cannot agree with. It will damage you more than anyone or anything else.

Dr. Shapero was educated at the University of Dayton (Ohio) and the U.S. Merchant Marine Academy (New York). He earned his doctorate at the Hebrew Union College (Cincinnati). His honorary doctorates are from the University of Dayton and the Hebrew Union College. In his spare time he is a licensed commercial pilot, avid sports enthusiast, and lover of opera and classical music. He is a Navy veteran and served in the U.S. Navy Chaplain Corps.

Chapter VII

What Really Matters at Work in Turbulent Times

(based on a presentation from Dr. Joan Marques, Dr. Satinder Dhiman, and Dr. Richard King at the Business Renaissance Institute on April 4, 2009)

When times are hard, opportunity knocks just as hard: we just forget to listen. This chapter discusses the troubles we face in difficult times, and reviews values and actions that can lead to a higher quality of life in spite of the problems. Through stories, examples, and reflections, the chapter will focus on imperative issues such as self-awareness, focusing on human capital, being value-based, refraining from sleep-walking, engaging in creative thinking and brainstorming, reaffirming our human values, being true to our ethical standards, and focusing on mutuality. Some valuable human-based behaviors will be endorsed, such as listening, telling the truth, reflecting on ourselves and focusing on the good instead of the bad, deviating from ethnocentrism, focusing on immaterial rather than material wealth, and helping one another.

Introduction

In recent years, we have faced some shocking collapses from companies that we though would be around forever. We also saw families and friends, who had great jobs, good incomes, and wonderful homes, lose overnight everything they worked so hard for. Hard times usually surprise us: They are an unexpected and unwelcome guest who clouds our view on life and robs us of our enthusiasm and perseverance. And yet, hard times can serve an important purpose.

This chapter focuses on hard times and the attitude we can adopt to get through them in the most graceful way. In the following sections, we will discuss the following themes:

1. Going backward to move forward

2. Creative thinking—no sleepwalking
3. Realignment of values

Going Backward to Move Forward

The great Swiss psychologist, Carl Gustav Jung once wrote a lengthy commentary on a Chinese Book of Life called *The Secret of the Golden Flower*. Speaking about the fundamental problems of life, Jung explained that people tend to learn to "outgrow" their problems by aligning themselves with some higher purpose: "Some higher or wider interest arose on the person's horizon, and through this widening of his view the insoluble problem lost its urgency. It was not solved logically in its own terms, but faded out when confronted with a new and stronger life-tendency."

Our Fundamental Values

In days of economic uncertainty and instability, the act of aligning ourselves to some "higher" interest is like going backwards to move forward. It simply means that we have to go back to our fundamental roots in order to harness untapped potentialities. For this to happen, we need greater self-awareness and self-knowledge. The following story illustrates the point well:

> *A traveler lost his way in a foreign land and eventually found himself in front of a tourist gift shop. The gift shop had all sorts of chapters for sale, from maps to travel guides to compasses. As the traveler was surveying the items displayed for sale, he was struck by rather a very unusual looking compass. This compass had a lid on it which, when opened, became a mirror. Intrigued by this unusual combination of compass and mirror, the traveler asked the lady on the sales desk: "I have seen all sort of compasses and mirrors; however, I have never seen them together. What is the purpose behind this strange combination? "Sir, the compass tells 'where' one is lost, while the mirror tells 'who' is lost!"*

This story splendidly illustrates the primacy of first finding out "who" is lost before attempting to solve problems. The tough times present the clarion call to take stock of our deeper aspirations, inner resources, and latent potential. "When it is dark," said Will Durant, "we can see the stars!" Difficult times are the perfect ones to find out what our true mission is, what our core values are, and what our unshakable principles are.

Principles Do Not Change: Know Them Well

During trying times, we need to stay true to our principles to regain our strength and courage. There is this interesting story, adopted from Steven Covey's book *Seven Habits of Highly Effective People:*

> *During one cold winter night, as one ship was sailing the raging waters of ocean, its captain felt that the ship had strayed from its normal sea route. Trying to get back on course, the captain spotted a dim flickering light, and wondered what it could be. The captain thought that it is might be another ship sailing towards them. So, he tried to communicate with the captain of this ship, stating to move out of the way. "We can't move" was the response, "because we are the lighthouse!"*

Invest in Human Capital

When we dig into any organizations deeply, we get people. It is all about people working with other people to accomplish some common goals. As Stanford professor Jeff Pieffer reminds us: People, not technology, build a great customer service program. Too often during tough times, we succumb to the temptation of laying off people in a bid to cut costs. These short-term savings are generally achieved at the future survival cost of the organization.

Know the Creative DNA of Your Organization

When we experience tough times, it becomes more important than ever to out-innovate our competition with creativity. Creativity is a function of high tolerance for mistakes combined with greater trust in the innovative powers of the rank and file. All the great ideas do not have to come from the top. Everyone can have a great idea. Great ideas don't discriminate. Therefore, we need to build efficient structures and utilize all our resources imaginatively. There is, for instance, a zoo in Canada that was having difficulty in disposing of animal waste. Thinking creatively, they packaged the animal pooh and creatively called it "Zoo-Do!"

Practice Value-based Servant Leadership

Servant leaders have a primary desire to serve a cause bigger than themselves. Tough times highlight both the good and bad aspects of leadership. The sole reason for the existence of the agency of leadership is to serve its constituents. There is no other justification. Life is like tennis: In order to win, one has to be good at service. If the institution of leadership is to survive, it has to take heart the message of selfless service. For only through service can we ennoble ourselves and glorify our existence. Albert Schweitzer once said, "I do not know what the future holds for you. But I am sure of one thing: only those of you will be happy who have found a way to serve. May we all be so fortunate."

Change Is Difficult: Habits Die Hard!

Why is change, which seems so intuitive, so hard to bring about? It is because we are creatures of habit. We like the comfort of the known and dislike the uncertainty of the unknown. And organizations are not any different from people. To illustrate his point about inveterate habits, let us look at the word "habit" itself. If we remove 'h' 'abit' remains. Remove 'a' 'bit' remains. And remove 'b' 'it' remains!

Let Your Life Speak

Gandhi reminds us to be the change we are trying to bring about in the world. We need to be careful how we live, for our life may be the only Bible some people will ever read. Here are two stories from Gandhi's life that illustrate his message splendidly:

> *A mother once brought her son to Mahatma Gandhi and said, "Sir, please tell my son to stop eating sugar."*
>
> *Gandhi looked at the boy for a long time and then, turning towards mother, said, "Bring your son back to me in two weeks."*
>
> *The mother did not understand the rationale of the delay in instruction, but she did as she was asked.*
>
> *Two weeks later she and her son returned. Gandhi looked deeply into boy's eyes and said, "Stop eating sugar."*
>
> *The mother was grateful, but puzzled. She asked, "Why didn't you tell my son to stop eating sugar two weeks ago when we were here?"*
>
> *And Gandhi replied, "Two weeks ago, I used to eat sugar myself."[1]*

The moral of the story is that we first need to discipline ourselves before we can try to discipline others.

Here is the second story, which says it all:

> *One day, when Mahatma Gandhi was boarding a train, one of his sandals slipped from his foot and landed near the track. Suddenly*

---

[1] Dan Millman, *Way of the Peaceful Warrior* (Tiburan, Calif.: Kramer, 1980)

the train began pulling away leaving him no time to retrieve it. Immediately, Gandhi removed the other sandal and tossed it back to lie with the other along the track. When his astonished fellow passenger asked why he did this, Gandhi replied, "Now the poor man who finds it will have a pair he can use."[2]

In challenging times, a simple act of compassion can mean more than a thoughtless gift.

Creative Thinking—No Sleepwalking

It is amazing when we look around us intensely, to see how many people are actually sleepwalking. "Sleepwalking" is what we do when we go through the motions, day after day, year after year, without really questioning ourselves. It's the mindless way of performing for a paycheck in order to pay the bills and hopefully have some extra spending money left. There is no awareness—no questioning—no real reflection on these activities.

A Positive Perspective on Hard Times

When hard times appear we are forced to wake up from our sleepwalk. Economic downturns, such as the one we experienced in the first decade of the twenty-first century, force us to re-evaluate our life, our career, and our directions for the future. Many of us have been laid off or know people who were. Some of us got reassigned at work, based on rightsizing and reformatting activities of our employers. And this was definitely not the only downturn we will experience. But we could view these downtimes in our lives as golden opportunities to end mediocre or even dreadful work relationships, which we might have held on to only because we happened to be in it and were too tired at the end of the day to think about the things we really wanted to do.

The *Times Tribune* from Scranton, PA, emphasized in one of its 2009 editions that successful people these days will be those who apply creativeness and stop doing what everybody else does. More specifically: the people who stop scanning the newspaper ads for more of the same that they have been doing in the past 10 or 20 years, and start to contemplate their own passions and creative skills. A great example of a person who looked around to focus on local needs was a Princeton college graduate who started a worm farm in 2009, in order to make nutrient-rich compost for gardeners. This young man

---

[2]In Steve Hagen, How the world can be the way it is: An inquiry for the New Millenium into Science, Philosophy, and Perception (Wheaton,Ill.: Quest Books), 300-301.

rented cheap warehouse space (which was abundantly available, because many stores and warehouses went out of business) and started collecting scraps from restaurants. "He surely didn't get a degree in worm farming, but he thought up an idea and made it work" (Nissley 2009).

A job-counselor who was interviewed in the article reviewed here admitted that many of the holdover jobs—from pest control to school bus drivers—are drying up now that more and more people lose their jobs. So it's the people who can think imaginatively that will be able to survive this recession in great shape (Nissley 2009).

The Power of Creative Thinking in Business

Creative thinking can make a world of difference in how we get through hard times. Here is an example of the advantage of creative thinking from an article on footwear, where it was revealed that shoe store owners in various parts of the country had decided to engage in something many of us haven't done in a long time: brainstorming. There was this shoe-store owner in Chicago, who, after talking things through with his employees, concluded that the local barbershop was the small-talk center of town. The shoe store engaged in a tie-in with the barber, granting him a free pair of shoes in exchange for a poster of the barber with the shoes on in his shop. Word of mouth did the rest. This is a classic example of the power of creative thinking in difficult times.

A Los Angeles shoe store also brainstormed with its employees: they received free shoes in exchange for serving as walking advertisements during work hours. The above examples disclose another high point in times of downturn: businesses collaborate more, internally and externally. Cutthroat envy is out—reciprocal favors are in again.

The Power of Creative Thinking at the Personal Level

In an article in the *National Law Journal,* the creativity problem was tackled at the personal level. It brought up something we should all consider seriously: three interesting reasons why working people don't often engage in creative thinking.

1. They feel that thinking is a passive pursuit. They claim that they are too busy to sit and think. There's nothing lazy or passive about thinking.
2. They confine their thinking to their work field, or they have learned to think within the boundaries of their daily tasks.

3. Many workplaces don't reward creative thinking. There are still many
    work environments –and bosses—who can get very displeased with
    out-of-the-box thinkers or healthy risk takers.

Aside from these top three problem areas toward creative thinking, there is
also the problem of peer pressure: we may want approval from our friends or
family, but if these people are traditionalists they will not encourage anything
out of the ordinary.

Finally, there are those self-imposed blockades that many of us maintain, such as self-esteem issues, or fear of what others may think of us. All
these mindsets prohibit us from wading into areas outside of our mental
comfort zone.

Here are three ways in which you can ignite creative thinking:

1. Engage in brainstorming sessions with friends who are proven
    creative thinkers. Ask them what they see in you. What skills and
    talents do they think you have? What areas can they envision
    you in? And of course, there are no bad ideas. Everything should
    be considered.
2. Look at yourself from the other side: what are employers looking for
    today? Try to put yourself in the shoes of various people you meet.
    Perhaps their job, their activity, their direction, may spark an idea
    within you that is useful toward your next career.
3. Consider the big picture. Take some distance. Step out of the daily
    routine, and go, if only for one day, to a place that inspires you. Places
    that break the daily rhythm also help open your mind and expand
    your horizons.

Encouraging our Inner Optimist

The poem below is titled "The Optimist and the Pessimist"

> *While part of me foresees near-future global integrations*
> *Another part fears endless wars and hatred between nations*
> *And while, on one hand, I truly enjoy the changing seasons*
> *I also whine and whimper about them for millions of reasons*
>
> *Some people know the art of being optimists in life:*
> *While others have the gift to change each act into a strife*
> *The zealots value pleasant sides of everything they see*
> *The doomsayers make sure they never once set their minds free*

Most of the time there's part of both in every one of us
Depending on our mindset we accept, or make a fuss
On happy days our glass is half full, and we celebrate
In gloomy times half empty, and we cry about our fate

It brings to mind two little boys with clear opposite views
One singing morning glory, while the other cried the blues
The optimist was dancing in the fertilizing rain
The pessimist just growled out that the dancer was insane

I bet you recognize yourself in each of these two lads
The cheerful one on sunny days; the drip on days with dreads
The wisest of advises, then, may be to dance life's twist
With open heart and mind toward our inner optimist

Realignment of Values

It remains painfully dramatic when we read about companies that handle downtimes in ways that are highly unspiritual. Some of these corporations are rather prominent in our society. Frequently, the companies determine the number and identities of employees who will be laid off but require strict secrecy about this until the time for the layoff has arrived. Meanwhile, human resources administrators have to act as if there is nothing wrong and display mandatory hypocritical behavior toward their colleagues. Then there are those that ask employees to check their ethics at the door before entering strategic sessions. All these corporate requirements are serious infringements on our personal values.

Reaffirming Our Values

What we need in the workplace during turbulent times is not so much a realignment of values, but a reaffirmation of our values, our ethical standards, and the fact that we cannot check our ethics at the door. Fortunately, it is not all doom and gloom. There are some hopeful developments, which indicate that a paradigm change is beginning to happen and that we are beginning to experience a business renaissance, or a greater sense of spirituality in the workplace. This new paradigm, and the consequential transformation, really started a number of years ago with 9/11, Enron, and Arthur Anderson, and most recently with AIG, Lehman Brothers, Bear Stearns, Madoff, bailouts, and a greed factor that has infected the business community.

New Perspectives on Work

Something is stirring in our souls for a more humanistic work environment, increased simplicity, more meaning, and a connection to something higher. Many people feel unappreciated, insecure, unhappy, and unfulfilled in their jobs—not only employees but executives at the highest level as well. People want to work in organizations that are mind-enriching, heart-fulfilling, soul-satisfying, and financially rewarding. People want to work in an environment where they don't have to check our values at the workplace door; they want a sense of "oneness." More and more people in the business world are turning inward and see a need for something bigger in life than just making money.

So, what does all this mean for those of us in business in turbulent times? It means that business must step up and adopt a tradition that we've never had throughout the entire history of capitalism. We must share responsibility for the "whole," for the planet and all it represents. We must focus on the quality of life rather than the quantity of life. We must move to new dimensions of thinking that encourage increased vision, creativity, caring, innovativeness, and ethical sensitivity. We must eliminate the barriers that we create and that prevent us tapping into the energy flow around us. We must eliminate this over reliance on extra gratification rather than internal development.

Many of the people involved in the recent scandals and government oversights are not inherently bad people. These people just lost their way. They got caught up in the need for external gratification and subsequently compromised their core values. As Bill George, retired chief executive officer of Medtronic, said, "They have lost their true north."

Actions Toward Business Renaissance

As part of the current paradigm change in business, we must pay more attention to stakeholders—customers, employees, the community, suppliers, and shareholders. We must try to develop a system in business that rewards our personal core values and creates a comfort zone where we can express and implement their values.

Here is some valuable advice from our first book, *Spirituality in the Workplace: What it Is, Why it Matters; How to Make it Work for You.* These suggestions may serve as guidelines regarding what we can do to help transform our workplace:

- Think of the positive and good things about all the people in your environment and the environment itself.

- Listen to suggestions from colleagues, because they might know something that you don't, and may even resolve a company problem.
- Maintain a positive attitude toward others, as well as yourself, because your attitude affects those around you.
- Treat others with respect and leave as much negativity as possible out of the workplace (including negative aspects of our personal life).
- Don't gossip. It is not pleasant to work where rumors circulate.
- Give credit when it is appropriate.
- Buy lunch for someone occasionally. What goes around comes around.
- Ask to cover for people, but don't let them take advantage.
- Mind your own business. Don't compare salaries.
- Smile!
- Do good (to stakeholders) while doing well (in leading the organization).
- Make your decisions in a dimension that reviews more than the bottom line, and consider enhancing the quality of life as a whole. When you do, the financial rewards will come automatically.
- Focus on developing relationships and facilitating people rather than merely producing a quantifiable product or service.
- Understand that motivating employees not only makes these employees feel better about themselves, it also increases their productivity.
- Understand the importance of family and try to allow your employees every opportunity to sustain a balance between the workplace and their personal lives.
- Be passionate about your work, and love what you do. Therefore, you should put your heart into it, and exude this contagious attitude toward your co-workers.
- Maintain high expectations for yourself as well as your co-workers; you should work hard yet keep your priorities in order; you should be firm, and even tough at times, but you should also be flexible and try to emphasize the positive while de-emphasizing the negatives.
- Stay away from toxic situations; you should do what it takes to keep your work environment as healthy as possible, so that employees can feel spiritually motivated to attend work.
- Treat others with respect and dignity, and you will find that you get treated in a similar way in return.

Turbulent times are filled with great opportunities. One of those great opportunities is to build a business climate that is nourishing and nurturing; not built on greed, fear, anxiety, and loss of confidence, but built on a system that emphasizes ethical behavior, inventiveness, and vision. A system where one's net worth is measured by one's contributions to the "whole," where the bottom line is more humane, and where we don't check our ethics at the door. What we should check at the door instead are greed, dishonesty, and toxic behavior.

Useful Insights for Turbulent Times

- While we should always try to see the best in everyone, we should also realize that there is a small percentage of human beings that is inherently bad. This small segment needs to be contained to prevent it from poisoning and taking advantage of the large percentage of innocent, well-intending individuals.
- In times when that there are many layoffs, people learn to start listening more to themselves instead of only to what others tell them. There need to be groups that assist people in creative thinking, and teach them not to stick to the status quo all the time.
- We need to "shoot straight," thus be truth tellers, when it comes to our behavior at work. This will help us as well as our co-workers feel better about the job, and set a good example to the world. In order to change the world, we have to start changing ourselves.
- We need to be cautious about the things we get charmed by. Many toxic leaders are captivating. We all have good and evil in us. Through reflection we can weed out the evil and ensure that we remain part of the large group of well-intending and compassionate, honest people.
- The crisis we have been experiencing in the past few years has opened our eyes to the ethnocentric mindset we nurtured for so long. We have come to realize now that, as a nation, we have flaws as well, which helps us realize that we don't stand out, but are an equal partner in an equal world.
- We have been mesmerized too long by the smoke from the genie bottle, but now we have come to realize that we should treat one another well, between individuals, but also between nations, regardless of status or economic position.
- Our current system is void of the safety measures that once kept ethics and values in place. Without these safeguards, greed has run rampant.

Yet, we should realize that wealth is not how much money you make, but whether you have the ability to have a job and a family.

- Human nature is not only about ethics but also about physics. The universe was not merely set up to accommodate our ways. We have not been able to eliminate wars and have created many problems along the way. If each person takes real responsibility for their actions, the percentage of "evil" persons will also get the urge to transform positively.

References

Covey, Stephen R. *The Seven Habits of Highly Effective People.* New York, NY: Simon & Schuster, 1989.

Lavine, Douglas S. "Creative Thinking." *National Law Journal* 31, no. 28 (2009): 13.

Nissley, Erin L. 2009. "Creative thinking goes long way." *Times-Tribune, The (Scranton, PA),* March 29. *Newspaper Source,* EBSCO*host* (accessed February 2, 2011).

Otey, Anne-Marie. "Creative Thinking." *Footwear News: FN* 65, no. 7:32.

Wilhelm, Richard, trans. *The Secret of the Golden Flower: A Chinese Book of Life.* (Comm. By C. G. Jung). New York, NY: Harvest Books, 1962.

Chapter VIII

Leader, Know Thyself: Crisis, Values, and Spirituality

(based on a presentation from Dr. Tim Kelly at the Business Renaissance Institute on June 20, 2009)

We all deal with crises sometimes. They surface at work, home, or elsewhere, usually at the least convenient moments. They also have a habit of pairing up, so that it seems as if they gang up on you. In this chapter, Dr. Tim Kelly reviews the phenomenon of crises. He explains that every crisis is actually a turning point, even though—or perhaps because—it creates great distress. A crisis provides us the opportunity to find out who we are and what we are about. The question, therefore, is, How can we manage the crises in our lives so that we can survive and come out better? Dr. Kelly reviews the concept of post-traumatic stress disorder and accentuates that we all suffer traumatic experiences at times, even if we are not immediately affected by the current economic crisis. There are three key resources that religion and spirituality provide for victims coping with trauma: 1) openness to religious or spiritual growth, 2) engagement in spiritual reflection, and 3) involvement in a faith-based community.

Crises and Our Responses to Them

It was not too long ago that we all experienced a massive economic crisis that continues to this day, but many of us are experiencing other crises as well—a crisis that may be in the personal arena, the professional arena, or both. While crises are usually seen (and experienced) as dreadful things, we can learn a lot from them. To set a positive tone, let's consider what President Obama's former chief of staff, Rahm Emmanuel, once stated: "A crisis is a terrible thing to waste." If you think about it, he's right: A crisis is always a potential turning point, even though—or perhaps because—it creates great distress. A crisis provides us the opportunity to find out who we are and what we are about. Crises can originate from many situations: divorce, illness, loss of a job, death, natural disasters, manmade disasters, combat, serious accidents, and so on. All of these factors can undo us, if we let them. The question is, therefore, How can we manage the crises in our lives so that we can survive and even come out the better for it?

The first thing we usually ask when hit by a crisis is, "Why me?" Subsequently, we may experience shock, anxiety, depression, hopelessness, and anger, but then we usually begin engaging in a desperate search for solutions.

One important question that people ask themselves in times of crises is, Where can I turn? Many of course turn to friends and family for comfort and support. But there are other resources to consider as well, especially one's faith and spirituality. If we can access these resources successfully, we can survive and even grow through crisis.

It is important to distinguish between spirituality and religion. Religion pertains more to an organized approach to believing in and praising a divine power, while spirituality is more geared toward an individual's personal expression of his or her search for meaning and purpose. Spirituality may or may not be found through organized religion. In times of crises, many people turn either to a deep sense of spirituality or to their faith-based community, which usually consists of a group of like-minded believers. This does not have to be an officially established congregation. It can also be an informal group of individuals with a similar perspective.

It is also important to understand the concept of post-traumatic stress disorder (PTSD), which applies to those who have experienced an overwhelming trauma and find afterward that they are simply unable to cope well with life's stressors. Economically dire times such as today's may have such an impact on people who lose their job, hence, their security, and find themselves having to start all over again—possibly losing all they worked for during many years. Consequently, we find that there are many people suffering from post-traumatic depression and other disorders triggered by the various traumas afflicting their lives.

We all suffer traumatic experiences at times, even if we are not immediately affected by the current economic crisis. Life happens to all of us. It is therefore important to learn how to manage personal and professional crises. Throughout crisis situations, we may find ourselves having the urge to withdraw, to talk less, or perhaps being overwhelmed by a sense of hopelessness. The burning question that arises is, Where do I go from here?

The good news is that if we look carefully at the experiences of those who have suffered from PTSD, we find that many of them ultimately grew from the trauma. For example, research has shown that many of the 9/11 survivors declared that despite their initial despair, their trauma eventually led to profound personal growth. They were able to make better interpersonal connections and understand others with more depth and compassion. They experienced positive changes in problematic interpersonal relationships, in life philosophy, and in their sense of peace and optimism in the face of adversity. The term "post-traumatic growth" is therefore starting to make headway in the analogs of clinicians and researchers.

Research has revealed three key resources that religion and spirituality provide to trauma victims that increase the likelihood of post-traumatic growth: 1) openness to religious or spiritual growth, 2) engagement in spiritual reflection, and 3) involvement in a faith-based community.

Regarding "openness to religious or spiritual growth," we must understand that there are two ways to respond to personal trauma: turning inward and holding on to grievances without releasing them, or focusing outward on one's understanding and openness to learn new things in the midst of suffering, which then leads to post-traumatic growth.

Regarding "engagement in spiritual reflection," there are also two ways to respond: On one hand, positive and productive approaches to spiritual reflection, and on the other, pointless rumination, which continues endlessly without conclusion. The former leads ultimately to ultimate growth, while the latter only enhances agony to the point of sheer despair.

Regarding "involvement in a faith-based community," a point of caution is in order: We should be careful not to get involved in a community that will harshly judge us for our mistakes and penalize us, making us even more miserable. The goal therefore is to find a group of like-minded people of faith and/or spirituality who will surround us with love and understanding and help us get on our feet again.

Crisis is a time for reflection change. We can benefit from asking ourselves three questions during hard times: 1) Who am I? 2) What do I believe in? 3) What do I want? The answers we find may surprise and empower us.

Crisis can help you grow in unexpected ways if you allow it. Crises usually prompt shifts in behavior, such as less time on the phone and more with loved ones; less speeding and more patience; less haste and more recognition of the importance of other people; less stress and more engagement in relaxing activities. Here are a few recommendations that position you to respond well to crisis:

1. Do not be satisfied with religious or spiritual beliefs that are rigid, unrealistic, and inflexible. Such beliefs will not help you cope well in time of crisis, and typically lead to self-condemnation rather than growth.
2. Regularly practice productive spiritual reflection, and do not wait for a crisis to do so. There are many ways to pursue this valuable experience, such as prayer, meditation, yoga, studying religious and/or spiritual writings, and so on.
3. Align yourself with a faith-based and/or spiritually oriented community that is capable of providing interpersonal support during times of crises.

Some Final Contemplations on Crises

Some readers might wonder what one should do when dealing with great trauma, when in fact they are not aware of any significant support system to fall back on. The answers to this question are as many as there are people and causes for trauma. But here is something to consider: If you keep your eyes open when coping with trauma you may meet someone who is affiliated with just such a support group. They tend to become more visible when we are in the midst of crisis. Such a person would likely be glad to invite you to his or her group, which may open wonderful doors for you. The key is to listen to your intuition and open up to people you trust. By doing this, and allowing others to come alongside you, you build up a community, even when you don't have immediate family or friends. If you are not a person likely to seek help from others, you may also find help in various readings from inspirational literature.

Many of us have endured the crisis and heartbreak of having to give up on a venture or relationship that was full of life, promise, and success. This can lead to a sense of disbelief as well as an array of symptoms that are hard to overcome, such as fear, a sense of failure, distrust, anger, depression, and the like. What we must realize at such times is that patience and an openness to change can lead to surprisingly positive outcomes. Losing a business or a great job or a dear relationship may be hard on the ego, yet it can also lead to insights and personal growth that would otherwise be unattainable, and that lead to a new flourishing.

Next time life inflicts crisis and trauma upon you, remember that a crisis is a terrible thing to waste.

Dr. Timothy A. Kelly currently serves as coordinator of behavioral health services and clinical psychologist for ParkwayHealth Medical Centers in Shanghai. A licensed clinical psychologist since 1990, he provides expert clinical care for adults, adolescents and couples struggling with emotional disorders. He specializes in cognitive-behavioral therapy (CBT), interpersonal psychodynamic therapy, and trauma-focused CBT. Dr. Kelly has served on the psychology faculties of several major universities, including Vanderbilt University in Tennessee and American University in Washington, DC. He is the author of *Healing the Broken Mind: Transforming America's Failed Mental Health System,* published by NYU Press in 2009. Dr. Kelly speaks, writes, and consults on how to achieve recovery-oriented mental health system reform. As director of the DePree Public Policy Institute, Dr. Kelly developed the concept of "principled centrism"—an alternative to polarizing extremism that has proven useful to local government and business leaders for problem-solving.

Chapter IX

Meditation for Busy Businesspeople

(based on a presentation from Dr. Joan Marques, Dr. Satinder Dhiman, and Dr. Richard King at the Business Renaissance Institute on October 17, 2009)

We don't need to read management books to realize that the pace of change has increased in the past few decades. Life has become more hectic than it has ever been. The demands that we face are forcing us to make ourselves more available more readily and through multiple communication channels. Increasingly, members of the corporate world realize that a break from this hectic lifestyle is not a luxury but a must, if we want to remain energetic, creative, and functional. It is therefore quite understandable that many business conferences, journals, and gatherings, include elements of meditation, yoga, and other mind-calming presentations and exercises. In this chapter, we share some experiences on meditation, in order to serve as an invitation to a more conscious way of living.

Meditation: Some Basics

Meditation has been around ever since human beings have. It is practiced in many different ways: with mantras, symbols, images, and different objects. It has been used for healing, calming, and awareness purposes, and with different focus points. Many people have meditated in some way or the other, at least once in their life. Meditation is not a religious practice per se. Rather, it's a psychological exercise that can be very helpful for busy people, whether they consider themselves Christian, Hindu, Muslim, Buddhist, atheist, agnostic, or anything else. In this chapter, we will focus our attention on our breath, one of the most widely used objects for meditation, followed by a simple guided mediation exercise.

Insight Meditation

The meditation technique that will be discussed in this chapter has proven particularly helpful for businesspeople. It is a technique that was revived in the twentieth century by a successful businessman from Burma, S.N. Goenka. Goenka earned a lot of money during his career as a businessperson, but, like most of us, he also struggled with a lot of stress. He was particularly troubled by severe migraine headaches. He tried everything to end his physical suffering, and finally came across a meditation teacher, who taught him Vipassana—the insight meditation. Goenka was so pleased with the results of Vipassana that he made it his mission to spread this technique on a global scale. Hence, we have numerous Goenka-style Vipassana meditation centers in every continent of the globe today.

Millions of businesspeople and other professionals, scholars, students, and homemakers around the world make time today to learn about Vipassana meditation. And yet, it is an ancient technique. It was rediscovered by Siddhartha Gautama, the Buddha, about 2,500 years ago. Having experienced both tremendous affluence and total abstinence, Siddhartha finally decided to practice this form of meditation in his search for ultimate truth in life. His attention naturally became stabilized on his breath and he discovered the answers to the fundamental questions of life in a state of total silence brought about by Vipassana, and subsequently taught this technique to many, until he died in his eighties.

Today, management scholars and businesspeople worldwide are starting to acknowledge the value of practicing Vipassana. At the recent annual conferences of the Academy of Management, several meditation-based workshops were offered; this may serve as an indicator that the need to find a technique to help us calm the mind is growing.

Raisin Exercise

A good exercise to start calming the mind and move toward greater mindfulness in the present moment is the raisin exercise. This exercise, which should take about five minutes, requires us to fully concentrate on the experience of eating a single piece of raisin. Those of us who like raisins usually throw a large number of them in our mouths and chew them all at once in a mindless manner. When engaging in the raisin exercise, we eat only one raisin, and it needs to happen with great attention and alertness. First of all, we focus on the texture, color, smell, and natural make-up of raisin. We try to engage all of sensory apparatus in "experiencing" the raisin in its full manifestation. This raisin should not be gulped in one bite, but in several slow, well-savored, and highly mindful bites. The raisin needs to be chewed carefully, and while doing so, we have to consider how many people have been involved in bringing this raisin to our hands: agrarians, harvesters, transporters, buyers, sellers, packers, producers of all materials, and everyone in between. We also need to consider all the work these people did, as well as all the things they needed to do this work: instruments, machines, and nature elements. This is an extensive cycle of efforts that we usually take for granted. Done sincerely, this may lead to an understanding how the whole universe had collaborated to make this raisin experience possible!

This exercise is useful, as it brings into scope the true interdependence of everything, thus the concept of "interbeing," as formulated by the Buddhist monk Venerable Thich Nhat Hanh.

Breathing Focus

In the five minutes that you devote to carefully eating the raisin, you will find your mind to be less rushed and slowly become calm and collected. Once in this state, you can begin the more in-depth calming of the mind: the breathing exercise. The breathing exercise can take as little as five minutes, but can be done for as long as you wish. For this purpose, it is important to sit in a relaxed position in which you can close your eyes. Once you have your eyes closed, you can start focusing on your breathing. However, you should avoid trying to control or regulate it. You should breath naturally just as you normally do, whether heavy or light, shallow or deep, long or short. Having done that for a few minutes, you could try to be aware which nostril is active at the moment of this exercise. Again, you should do this without trying to manipulate the process of breathing in any form or shape. Just remain aware of your pure, natural, effortless breath as you watch its movements. All you need to do is to observe and to refrain from getting aggravated or excited in any way.

Guided Meditation

With this five-minute (or longer) breathing exercise as foundation, you can now start your own insight meditation session. Be aware of the fact that this may not be as easy as it seems in the first few attempts, especially when you're doing this alone. Many busy businesspeople may find their mind wandering off repeatedly and may have a hard time calming their minds in any way.

During the initial sessions it may be useful to include a short break if you feel that you need to get up. If you attempt this exercise along with others and you need to get up, try to do so as quietly as possible, so that you don't disturb your fellow meditators. A session may last for as long as you feel comfortable. Most busy businesspeople spend anywhere from 30 minutes to one hour on such a meditation session.

Focus Points During the Session

During the meditation session, you can engage in a mental body scan, in which you concentrate on each aspect of your body and try to examine it with no emotional attachment. Do not get upset when you find that your mind has been wandering for awhile, because this is a perfectly common occurrence, especially for first-timers. Just notice that your mind has wandered away and try to bring it back gently, first to be aware of your breath and then to the movement of your attention as it travels throughout your body from head to toe.

The body observation process has to happen very slowly, starting from the top of the head, and sliding down ever so slowly over the face, chest, abdomen, back, arms, thighs, lower legs, and feet, and then up again to the top. Once the slow scanning cycle is completed, you may start again, from the top down, and then up again. The purpose of this body scanning process can be explained as follows:

> *Vipassana, or insight meditation, is a way of self-transformation through self-observation. It focuses on the deep interconnection between mind and body, which can be experienced directly by disciplined attention to the physical sensations that form the life of the body, and that continuously interconnect and condition the life of the mind. It is this observation-based, self-exploratory journey to the common root of mind and body that dissolves mental impurity, resulting in a balanced mind full of love and compassion (Vipassana Meditation, 2009).*

There is much to be found on the Internet about Vipassana meditation. There are complete guidelines, and there are many retreat locations all over the world for those who would like to try it. Having engaged in Vipassana meditation as well, we, the authors of this chapter, warmly recommend it as a way of calming the mind and attaining a more realistic, reasonable, and peaceful perspective on life.

Opinions of Busy Businesspeople on Vipassana

Many busy corporate workers may not succeed in the first sitting to calm the mind for a reasonable amount of time, or even concentrate optimally on the body scanning process. Put simply, Vipassana is way of "minding our mind." Our mind seems to have a mind of its own and will find countless ways to distract us from calming it. It will bring up all kinds of thoughts that we had not entertained for a long time: songs, people, places, things people said, things to do, the past, the future, and many more. Mind likes to be elsewhere and freely oscillates between future hopes and past memories, without ever remaining in the eternal Now. The art is to gently bring the mind back to the here and now and continue the scanning process as soon as we become aware of the distraction. If we do so often enough, we will gain control again over our mind, and acquire the art of calming it.

While full and continued concentration may be hard at first, most people agree that they feel a higher level of internal serenity, even after the first exercise. Due to the different levels of readiness we all have, some of us may find it easier than others to continue the meditation process in one sitting. Even at a first effort, some people manage to refrain from giving in to the impulse of getting up, while others will find it extremely hard to sit still and may even fail to understand the philosophy behind meditation sessions as a means of improved performance and quality of life. This may be attributed to the different levels of readiness within us to explore this degree of tranquility. Those who have a hard time with meditating may feel that they are dealing with a wide cultural gap in practices and that they would much rather engage in other activities such as walks, tours, or other alternatives to step out of the daily hustle and bustle. This, too, is understandable, because different people appreciate different ways of performing, thinking, working, relaxing, and rejuvenating, and this should be respected.

As an endnote, we emphasize that members of the workforce should be offered various options to release their stress, so that they can attain better results and more gratification from their work and enjoy higher levels of personal and professional well-being. Vipassana is just one of the many ways available to calm the mind and to lead us to greater awareness.

Reference

"Vipassana Meditation." http://www.dhamma.org/en/vipassana.shtml
    Accessed January 21, 2010.

Chapter X

Exploring the Link Between Spirituality and Sustainability

(based on an interactive potluck-based presentation at the Business Renaissance Institute on February 20, 2010)

In the first decade of the twenty-first century, some words came to the forefront of our attention. Two of these words are sustainability and spirituality. The reasons are obvious: as we deal with increasing dissatisfaction, corporate greed, and alarming newscasts about environmental degradation, we are seeking a proper response to restore, or even improve, a sense of meaning and purpose, in order to work toward overall well-being for all of life on earth. The focus of this chapter is to clarify the link between spirituality and sustainability. The focus points will vary from implementing in daily activities spiritual practices that contribute to a more sustainable environment, to deviating from selfishness, becoming aware of the need to empathize more and demand less, considering long-term effects on short-term actions, replacing victimhood with infinite being, replacing mutual criticism with constructive community thinking, and learning from the ever-creating and balancing wholesomeness of nature.

From "Me" to "We": Expanding Our Daily Sense of Responsibility

> *"Our prime purpose in this life is to help others. And if you can't help them, at least don't hurt them." —The Dalai Lama*

One way to perceive the link between spirituality and sustainability is this straightforward one: these two phenomena cannot exist without each other! You cannot be a spiritual person without contributing to a sustainable environment, and there cannot be a sustainable environment without spiritual people. Jonas Salk, an American medical researcher and virologist, once said, "If all the insects were to disappear from the earth, within 50 years all life on earth would end. If all human beings disappeared from the earth, within 50 years all forms of life would flourish." Dr. Salk's statement places an emphasis on the fact that we human beings need to shift our thinking and, subsequently, our actions toward a flourishing natural environment, *even with* our presence. And why would this not be possible? After all, we are intelligent beings, and we have the ability to wake ourselves up by consciously reviewing the problems we have created thus far. One of our major problems in the world is poverty. However, poverty is a human-made problem. So too are global warming, excessive pollution, irresponsible occupation, and destruction of rainforests. In other words, the entire ecological imbalance that we are currently witnessing consists of human-caused problems. When we look at the picture from a macro level, we could easily get disheartened and shrug the whole thing off as a hopeless situation. Yet, we can all make a difference at the micro level: from our own little place, wherever that may be.

Daily Acts toward Greater Sustainability

There are numerous ways in which we can contribute to a more sustainable environment. These are small and certainly not new ways, but every little bit helps:

- Turn off the lights when you leave a room, even if you are not the one who pays the energy bill.
- Close the tap while brushing your teeth, even when you are not the one to pay the water bill.
- Correct little wrongs, such as picking up a bottle that dangerously lies in a parking lot and can cause harm to car tires, even if you were not the one who placed it there; or place an item back in the right place in the store where you shop, if it doesn't take too much of your time— even if you are not the one who left it in the wrong place.

When we engage in these small actions, we are not only acting in favor of sustainability; we are also doing the spiritually right thing. Our individual contribution toward linking spirituality and sustainability could be expressed in simple acts such as assisting other people, even if we don't have to; being kind toward all living beings, even if we don't know them; and refraining from participating in any kind of mean-spirited behavior, even if we could legally justify it.

Sustainability includes the ability to sustain values such as love, purpose, meaning, goodness, happiness, peace, and life. Spirituality, on the other hand, lies in our engagement in acts of sustaining love, purpose, meaning, goodness, happiness, peace, and life. Realizing the link between spirituality and sustainability starts with stepping away from a "me" mindset, and adopting the natural "we" mindset that many of us seem to have forgotten: realizing the value of our left-brain intelligence, but combining it with our right-brain awareness, which underscores our interconnectedness.

It is easy to say, "I can't do anything about these large-scale problems. I didn't create them. This is something for businesses and governments." Yet, we should rethink that mentality and realize that we can all make a difference, regardless of how small the scale. To illustrate how this mindset works, here the story of the *Star Thrower*, published by Loren Eiseley in 1969:

> *One day a man was walking along the beach when he noticed a boy picking something up and gently throwing it into the ocean. Approaching the boy, he asked, "What are you doing?" The youth replied, "Throwing starfish back into the ocean. The surf is up and the tide is going out. If I don't throw them back, they'll die." "Son," the man said, "don't you realize there are miles and miles of beach and hundreds of starfish? You can't make a difference!" After listening politely, the boy bent down, picked up another starfish, and threw it back into the surf. Then, smiling at the man, he said, "I just made a difference for that one."*

Measuring Our Growth by Our Distance from "Self" Thinking

> *"After being a student of human life and history, I conclude we just have to be a bit kinder to each other. We have to achieve freedom from the disability called egotism." —Aldous Huxley*

The natural proposal consists of self-preservation and self-replication of the species. Unfortunately, human beings have become too hung up on these two aspects, especially the "self" part. It is now, more than ever, important to be aware of our actions and thoughts. There is a statement from the Dalai Lama that goes like this: "I need to root out the anger and hatred from my heart in order to help my people." In spite of the insights that many wise people have shared with us, the main problem with humanity is self-interest, which some of us now conveniently refer to as "enlightened self-interest." This demonstrates how quick we are to find beautiful ways of wrapping all our actions and justifying them in our minds. Another example is our eloquent rephrasing of the problem of "too much debts," which we now refer to as "highly leveraged." If we take a critical look at all theories we learn throughout our education, we can see how the self-serving mindset is solidified within us. Even in Maslow's famous hierarchy of needs, the distinctive egoistic needs have been renamed to "self-esteem."

Here is a story that wonderfully captures the problem of our contemporary frame of mind. This story may serve as an eye-opener toward giving the gift of harmlessness at the spiritual core:

> *There was a wealthy man who had invested much of his money in a luxury mansion. Life was going well, but one day, while at work, the man learned that his mansion was on fire. He became overwhelmed with all kinds of downtrodden emotions: sadness, anger, disbelief, despair, and the like. His eldest son came into his office and the man cried to his son, "Have you heard? The mansion is on fire!" Upon which the eldest son soothingly said, "Don't worry, Dad, we sold it last week. Don't you remember? The problem is not ours!" The man was relieved and resumed his daily task. But then his youngest son came in and said, "Dad, the house is on fire and we have not received the payment for it yet!" The father, once again, became desperate and sad, upon which his middle son came in and said, "Dad, don't worry. The payment was wired to us yesterday!"*

The story above illustrates the mindset of many members of contemporary society: we always think of our own well-being and how things could benefit us, and don't worry about others' troubles. Albert Einstein once said, "You measure the growth of a person depending on his or her distance from 'self' thinking." We are still too deeply stuck in the mentality of "Thank God, it's not me," a mindset that is detrimental to the collective well-being. It is only when we get rid of the self-interest plague that we can become uplifted and start to understand the link between spirituality and sustainability.

Tuning Our Brains Into What Our Heart Is Already Telling Us

When we perceive the trends of the past decades from a brighter angle, we discover that we are gradually moving toward a greater emphasis on the quality of life than the quantity of life. Here are some simple examples:

Less than a year ago, one of the authors of this chapter had a meeting with Dr. Mike Yamano, founder and chancellor of the Yamano College of Aesthetics, during which they discussed the topic of enhancing the quality of life for older women in Japan. Dr. Yamano described how his school of cosmetology brought in and enhanced the quality of life of women from nursing homes and assisted-living facilities. In an effort to link the best of East and West, the author introduced leaders of the USC Davis School of Gerontology to those of Tokyo University, igniting a collaboration for teaching gerontology in Japan, the country with the world's oldest living population. This collaborative link should not be seen only at its immediate, micro level, but even more in the value of constructive collaboration between education systems from East and West.

There are several other ventures that people engage in these days that attest to greater awareness levels. The very fact that we now have the phenomenon of social entrepreneurs, who maintain the entrepreneurial mindset but focus on general well-being. This explains the rise of businesses that focus on going green, enhancing awareness, and offering microcredits to the poor.

Our Common Aspects

An interesting perspective on the link between spirituality and sustainability is this one: We, human beings, have two important things in common, life and death. We are therefore connected in ways we often don't consider. Instead of focusing on our differences, we should rethink the need for supporting each other and, as a consequence, ourselves. The Norwegians consider empathy the right approach toward other human beings; unfortunately, this phenomenon has not yet nestled itself into the human community. We could see our connection in many things, in the fact that most of us work, have the capacity for suffering, have the will to move toward self-realization, deal with skepticism of the status quo, and face the effects of globalization. Human communication has increased tremendously through advanced information technology, and many members of the younger generations of today communicate vividly through Internet-based social entities such as Facebook and Twitter with friends they have yet to meet. These younger people seem to be on the right path in breaking racial, cultural, and geographical barriers by embracing friends worldwide. The older generation should consider adopting some of these advantages in embracing others, so that the segregative mindset that leads to excessive self-focus is conquered.

Earth As a Living Being

It is no secret that our planet is a living being and that our individual practices are continuously affecting the biosphere. On the mystic side, we should shift from our telescope mentality, looking outward, to looking inward and realizing that we have an internal eco-system that harmonizes with the external atmosphere. We therefore need to consider both the internal and external states of affairs to attain greater quality of life, consisting of internal and external harmony.

Enhanced Consciousness

We could consider replacing the term *spirituality* with *consciousness*. We can then make it our goal to sustain or enhance our level of consciousness, which is possible in several ways, including:

1. Looking at the end before beginning
2. Reconsidering your story and replacing victimhood with infinite being, leaving behind a lot of depressing baggage that could be an impediment to full functioning in an interconnected world
3. Living in the present to ensure greater sustainability of your spiritual life. Guilt about the past and fear of the future will hold us at the level of followers, and getting rid of these negative emotions can elevate us beyond the desire to win and will allow us to be ourselves more. It boils down to becoming able to say less "no" to others, and less "yes" to yourself.
4. Experiencing the world as a group of communities instead of 6 billion beings, and shifting back to the mindset that used to exist in hunter-gatherer communities: more equality, thus healthier societies

Focus on Common Values

Yet another perspective of connecting spirituality and sustainability is to strive toward greater acceptance and less criticism among religions. Many people affiliate themselves with these mindsets, which don't lead to constructive community-thinking. Religious leaders should elevate themselves beyond these separating standards and shift toward their common values of goodness, support, and acceptance.

Respecting Nature

Respect of nature is another important link between spirituality and sustainability. We could learn a lot from nature, where everything is in balance. We should respect that but have not done so until now. We don't nurture and appreciate the gift of our body, for instance. When we take the time to study nature, we can learn much about helping others—and ourselves—by refraining from disrupting rhythms and redirecting everything. Spirituality and sustainability begin with respect of life—our own lives and the lives of others. Nature is not wasteful. It keeps creating. The more we learn that, the more empathy we will build up; and the more intelligently we act, the more aware we will be of the simple things that we do that have such tremendous consequences.

Interhuman Connection

Spirituality could be explained in multiple ways, varying from metaphysics to the role in cultures. In our spiritual thinking, we should move from short-term to long-term thinking. We could raise many questions about over-focus on self and over-focus on non-self, but human values such as quality, humility, passion, diligence, mindfulness, faith, civility, and insight should be our leading motives in today's corporate behavior. Many might not identify these values as spiritual values, but whether they do so or not, these values are crucial to our interhuman connection; they lead to sustainability in cultures and humans, as well as sustainability of the self.

Chapter XI

Journey Back to Spirituality

(based on a presentation by Kathleen Stillwell, RN, MPA/HSA, CPHRM, at the Business Renaissance Institute on May 22, 2010)

This chapter presents a touching spiritual reflection of a busy female executive who reconnected with her spirituality after a near-destructive crucible in her life. In a spiritual audit of her life, Kathleen Stillwell shares a story that many working people can relate to: a story of conventional success that is overshadowed by a sense of purposelessness that begs to be fulfilled. Kathleen then explains how a major loss in her life ultimately caused her to refocus and discover the meaning that so many of us let go astray.

Life As an Immaculate Stream

Kathleen Stillwell lived the life that many people dream of: she was healthy, enjoyed a wonderful youth, married young, and happily created a family that included a bright and beautiful daughter and son. She enjoyed a very successful career and worked herself up to financial security. Yet, as her youth transformed into maturity, she experienced a growing sense of restlessness and began to question purpose in her mind. She started wondering if work is all there is to life. While her own search for meaning became increasingly obvious to her, Kathleen could not exactly point to any specific problem; she just felt that something seemed to be missing. Meanwhile, she kept doing what she knew best: business-traveling and consulting for health care, tending to her family, and practicing her Christian faith.

The Call That Changed Everything

Near midnight, on January, 16 1999, Kathleen received a call that her son, Nathan, who was traveling with his university in Mexico, had been critically injured in an accident and rushed to a local Red Cross clinic. Given her nursing background, she understood the serious nature of his injuries and immediately started placing calls, spending the next four hours arranging a medical charter jet to fly Nathan back to the United States for medical care. Nathan, 23 years old, had sustained severe life-threatening injuries, including chest and head trauma, and was airlifted to Houston, TX. Despite heroic medical efforts, multiple surgeries, and the finest medical care available, Nathan's clinical condition continued to deteriorate. This young man, always so vibrant and full of life, was being kept alive artificially. By his seventh day in the intensive care unit the physicians and the family realized there was no hope that Nathan would recover from his injuries or regain cognitive functioning.

Kathleen had to make the most difficult decision a mother ever has to make: to discontinue life support on her only son. As she watched the heartbeat of her beloved son cease, Kathleen felt her own spirit drain out of her. At that moment she felt the escape of her faith, joy, and interest in the life surrounding her.

Work, Work, Work

In the years immediately following Nathan's passing, Kathleen buried herself even deeper in her work. She stopped going to church, as she had lost her faith, and shut herself off emotionally. Her business life surged and her "success," as it is defined conventionally, skyrocketed. Work seemed to be the only place where she could function, so that's what she did. She relentlessly devoted almost all of her time to her career. She loved her work and found a sense of gratification in it. Even though she was near the point of exhaustion, she continued pushing herself, because even if she felt numb and felt empty, work seemed to be a safe place. When we lose something near and dear in our personal life, we often do just that: cling to our work to hide from the pain and grief that would otherwise overwhelm and drown us.

Like so many of us, Kathleen did not know how to deal with the loss of spirit she experienced. Yes, she still had a loving daughter, a husband, and friends, but she could not allow herself to feel any better. She worked and traveled in search for meaning, now even more than ever before. China, Russia, Switzerland, Paris, Italy, working in wonderful places all over the world: They were great, but could not fill the emotional gap. She wrote journals, which she never read. She needed to get her thoughts out but did not want to face them. She struggled with her emptiness, and her family was at a loss as to coping with this behavior. Kathleen was also at a loss. She realized the importance of valuing what she still had and engaging in the things she had enjoyed in life before Nathan's death. But she could not seem to extend her world past the work that consumed her days.

Small Steps Toward Meaning

About two years after the tremendous crucible, Kathleen's daughter decided that she wanted to renew her faith. She started attending a contemporary, charismatic church and urged Kathleen to accompany her. The church was contemporary, filled with spirit and music. Being a music lover, Kathleen liked the atmosphere; she joined the church with her daughter but was not sure she was really feeling the spirit. Sometimes it felt like she was going through the motions more than being there fully.

The church offered an evening program for bereaved parents who had lost a child. The program was not a church program but was sponsored by a hospice organization and held at the church campus. Kathleen attended the program weekly for 16 weeks, accompanied by her sister-in-law. During each session six to 10 bereaved parents would share their stories of loss and heartbreak with one another. Kathleen started sharing during these meetings with people who had been struck by a similar painful loss. As she gradually started opening up, she realized that in the past two years she had not fully dealt with her own loss of her son.

Yet, even as she allowed herself to be more open and vulnerable to people, she regularly hid in a book when traveling for her work. Then, one day, during a flight to yet another business meeting, she came to sit beside an older gentleman who refused to fall for the "don't bother me, I'm reading" trick. The man wanted to engage in a conversation, and asked Kathleen how many children she had. She thought for a moment and then answered, "Two. One on earth and one in heaven." While this might have silenced other people, the man did not stop there. He said, "How sad! Tell me about what happened to the one in heaven." And Kathleen opened up. She told her entire story, for the first time, to this stranger. It felt good to talk. A few days later, the man sent her an e-mail, thanking her for her trust and sharing with her his own loss: his brother had also lost a son, so he could vividly relate to everything she had been going through.

Life Has Meaning

As Kathleen learned to open up again to life, she increasingly started to enjoy the things that really mattered. She came to understand that the deep pain and sorrow of her loss was also a measurement that paralleled the depth of her love for the son she had lost. Her daughter married and had a son. The first grandson brought new light to Kathleen's life as she realized a deep joy for the first time since Nathan had died. Life seemed filled with a new magic. Her family established an endowed scholarship in Nathan's name at his university, and her daughter and son-in-law commemorated Nathan's passing by dedicating a park bench that carries Nathan's name. Kathleen makes it a point to regularly sit on this bench with her grandchildren, who enjoy "Uncle Nathan's Bench."

Kathleen reduced her workload in order to devote more time to her family and social life. And last year, after 10 years untouched, Nathan's bedroom was turned into a useful space in their home. To acknowledge the 10-year anniversary of Nathan's passing, Kathleen had beautiful memory bears made from several articles of Nathan's clothing. The bears were given to family members in memory of a dear loved one who no longer was among them … but was never forgotten.

From the Outside In: Contemplating Kathleen's Story

Kathleen's revelation is one that touches the hearts of many, especially those who have experienced losses in their lives and know the sense of emptiness that this brings about. When we think of our crucibles, which come in many shapes and sizes, we realize that they serve an important purpose in our lives. Through the pain they cause, they teach us to refocus on the things that really matter: human connection, happiness, and contentment, rather than financial affluence, popularity, and splendor. While the latter are nice assets, they are unable to provide us with a sense of purpose in life's journey. Too many people lose focus and bury themselves in a cycle of work and achievement, competition, and a win-lose strategy.

Kathleen's courageous act of sharing her touching life story may present the readers of this book, whether business executives, academics, students, entrepreneurs, or corporate employees, with the reality that there are some things that all the money, acclaim, and job titles can't buy: peace and joy after the loss of a dearly loved one. Yet, one doesn't have to lose a loved one to attain this awareness. As human beings, we have the ability to understand and relate, and we can deduce from the experiences of others that life can be beautiful and that we have the shape and content of our lives in our own hands. It's up to us, how we want to furnish it.

Kathleen Stilwell is the patient safety risk management account executive for The Doctors Company. Her experience includes risk management, professional liability claims management, regulatory compliance, and governance of health care services. With 29 years' experience in the health care industry, Kathleen is recognized as an expert in developing collaborative relationships with providers, purchasers, and liaison with community agencies. She has held senior executive positions with major health care organizations in the United States, has consulted nationwide on health care risk management and professional liability claims issues, and held adjunct faculty positions with the University of San Francisco, Woodbury University, and the American Society of Health Care Risk Managers. She is published in risk management and quality and has presented more than 1,000 seminars on risk management and related issues for United States and international audiences. Kathleen is a registered nurse, with a bachelor's degree in English and master's degrees in public administration and health services administration.

Chapter XII

East Meets West: Best Business Practices in Light of a New Spirituality

(based on a presentation from John Krysko at the Business Renaissance Institute on August 21, 2010)

While the discrepancy between East and West seems major, it is actually nonexistent. In a fascinating journey through time, John Krysko underscores that we need to seriously consider adopting a different mindset than the one we have mainly adhered to up till now: thinking in terms of "us vs. them" has been the cause of many troubles in human existence. Unfortunately, we have misinterpreted those who have tried time and again to educate us. Krysko travels through time, continents, and cultures to support his viewpoints. He weaves an interconnected web of human performance, highlighting the need to re-evaluate the messages that we thought we understood so far but have obviously misinterpreted.

East Is East and West Is West

The first sentence in Rudyard Kipling's "The Ballad of East and West" is:

> "Oh, East is East, and West is West, and never the twain shall meet."

One who does not read further will find easy confirmation for a thought that many hold: there is an unbridgeable gap in cultures and ideologies and human beings will never unite. Yet, when one reads the rest of Kipling's poem, it becomes obvious that, true to his consistently manifested wisdom, he concludes that East and West *do* unite and that there is actually *no difference:*

Onward to a New Spirituality

Leibniz's Philosophies

When we think about a new spirituality we first need to take a few steps back in time, and a great starting point is the seventeenth-century philosopher Gottfried Withelm Leibniz (1646-1716). Leibniz was a jurist, mathematician, diplomat, historian, theologian of no mean proportions, and Germany's greatest seventeenth-century philosopher. Dunes (1942) describes Leibniz as "one of the most universal minds of all times." Leibniz had personal contact with other great contemporary thinkers such as Newton, Boyle, and Spinoza. Leibniz developed the infinitesimal calculus independently of Isaac Newton, and his mathematical notation has been widely used ever since it was published. Leibniz also developed the binary number system, which is at the foundation of virtually all digital computers.

As a philosopher, Leibniz is best known for writing *The Monadology* and developing the theory of the pre-established harmony. Both of these underscore the law of causality, which is heavily underscored by Buddhists in our times. In simple wording, Leibniz believed that everything exists for a reason, and, similarly, that nothing arises for no reason. In his theory of pre-established harmony he clarifies his understanding of causality that every "substance" only affects itself, but all the substances (both bodies and minds) seem to causally interact with each other because they harmonize with each other.

Leibniz is best known for his broadminded approach, which can be confirmed by the fact that he acknowledged Newtonian thinking but also identified with the Eastern teachings of Mencius and Confucius. According to Leibniz, the Eastern moral and ethical philosophy was superior to the Western. He was profoundly impacted by this awareness and realized that it was not very different from his own deliberations on spirituality. Leibniz felt that the Eastern moral directions should be observed in order to refrain from going astray. This was not merely Leibniz's theory; he practiced it as well. Leibniz should be applauded for his pre-Einstein awareness of the fact that there is no division between business and spirituality.

Spirituality in Contemporary Business

Perhaps it should be advocated that a study of spirituality (as a work-related value) become a steadfast part of every MBA program, so that business students would be instilled with proper values prior to their engagement in the corporate world. Duty is important, but even more so is the development of oneself. In a world without moral directives, we get confronted with augmented selfishness, short-term focus, and a blatant disregard for those outside of our immediate environment. This is not due to the lack of external rules and regulations, but rather to the lack of an internal moral compass. It would help the business community as well as uplift the human condition if we could realize that the real law we all adhere to resides inside. That is the law to listen to. As Mencius, the great student of Confucianism living in the fourth century BC, stated: "Every duty is a charge, but the charge of oneself is the root of all others."

The Chinese and the Greek

In order to link Leibniz's theories to Confucian philosophy, it might be profitable to reconsider the case of China as a superpower that has rapidly evolved to become the second-largest economy in the world. Yet, China went through its share of struggle and strife. Glancing back to the days of Confucius, we can read about the desperation that his students felt at the time of the Master's death. The era of the "Warring States" was just starting, and the students asked Confucius what they should do. Their teacher just pointed to the stars and stated that the answers lie in there, because everything happens as it should.

Internal morality and the law of causation are also recurring themes that one can find not only in Sun Tzu's *The Art of War,* but also in Greek philosophy. Although it was written during the Warring States Period, when Confucian moral values and social connectivity had broken down, *The Art of War* upholds the importance of maintaining a values-based approach to conduct. According to Sun Tzu, knowing yourself as well as your enemies would "enable you to win 100 wars without a single fight." The Greek notion "know thyself" pertains not only to knowing ourselves individually, but also knowing others as interconnected parts of our existence. Hence, all above described philosophers and their works draw us back to this immensely important insight: We cannot view ourselves separate from other beings. Our destinies are interconnected.

And yet, humanity has made error upon error throughout its existence through incomplete understanding and partial interpretation of the above theories. It becomes obvious through a study of the strategies of Mao Zedong, the successes and failures of Gen. Douglas MacArthur, the ultimate futility of the Great Wall of China, and short-sighted contemporary business practices. When a group starts perceiving itself as an entity separate from others, all theories get a different meaning, and this can lead to the outcomes we have witnessed.

Theory Z

Perceived in light of organizational performance, it is important for the link to be confirmed in this chapter, to consider Theory Z, which is often credited to William Ouchi but was initially developed by the psychologist and human potential pioneer Abraham Maslow. The forerunner of this theory is McGregor's Theory X and Y, in which Theory X managers consider their employees lazy and in opposition to the company's progress, thus cannot be trusted while Theory Y managers consider them to be reasonable, trustworthy human beings who want the best for the company.

Theory Z, whether considered from Maslow's or Ouchi's perspective, deviates from McGregor's theory in that it does not view matters from the managerial perspective as McGregor's theories X and Y do, but from the employee's standpoint. In Maslow's perspective, "Theory Z places more reliance on the attitude and responsibilities of the workers" ("Maslow's Theory Z").

In Theory Z, Maslow described a new type of person resembling the 1-in-100 form of self-actualizer. This type was called the *transcender*. Transcenders were people who consciously built the characteristics of peak experiences into everyday life." (Dewey 2007).

In the 1980s, when the United States was going through a managerial downturn, William Ouchi presented his Theory Z. "Ouchi's Theory Z advocates a combination of the best of theory Y and modern Japanese management, placing a large amount of freedom and trust with workers, and assumes that workers have a strong loyalty and interest in team-working and the organization" ("Maslow's Theory Z"). Ouchi also examines the corporate philosophies that have become blueprints for Theory Z success, and looks at the evolving culture of "Z" people in society (Ouchi).

Whether Maslow's or Ouchi's domain, Theory Z posits that employees are total human beings who can contribute significantly and should be respected as such. Theory Z gives us hope that there can be a positive interchange and that good ideas don't just have to come from top management, but can come from all sides if acknowledged.

Theory Z is much in line with the mindset of ownership for all participants, which is also presented in Sun Tzu's *The Art of War,* which asserts that man cannot be a master tactician if not able to deal with chaos and think on his feet. As relayed before, this mindset recurs through history. The Greeks understood it well and taught it in their mystery schools: there is a relationship between the "predictable" and the "unpredictable," and this reality can be found in practically all disciplines.

Some Final Contemplations on a New Spirituality

Our Relationship With God

Some people wonder, how we, as we appear to live as temporal beings, could be related to God. A good way to start explaining this is as follows: Our intellect has adopted a square-based thinking pattern. Yet, if you break a square down infinitely, you arrive at a circle. We seem to have forgotten our "circleness" and are caught in the square-based thinking pattern. Oftentimes we pay lip service by making spirituality-based statements of interconnectedness, while many of us are still trapped in this square-based mindset. The sole goal of the universe is to raise our consciousness. Leibniz saw this in his calculus theories: There is a link between mathematical thinking and holistic thinking. Newton did not get to that level and remained at the divisive mindset, which we have broadly adopted in our Western-based thinking and acting of the past centuries. Yet, we all have the ability to rise above the square mindset, and we should strive to attain this consciousness. We will then come to terms with our infiniteness. We are more than our intellect and our intuition. We are the likeness of God, and have it all in us. We can learn much from other cultures, such as the African Ubuntu, an ethic or humanist philosophy that focuses on human beings' allegiances and relations with each other. Ubuntu means, "I am what I am because of who we all are." This concept teaches that the whole world is one single family and that we can work out our differences in peace.

Individualism vs. Collectivism

Some people, especially those who were born and raised in individualistic societies such as that of the United States, may have some trouble with the idea of interconnectedness being proclaimed in this chapter. They may hold that the United States was built by independent people who created a system that has worked well so far. They may therefore become defensive and feel that it is a bit far-fetched to challenge the quality of life in the individualistic U.S. society and adopt Eastern, collectivist ways.

The answer to this fear could be found along the lines of Einstein's statement that *"Problems cannot be solved at the same level* of awareness that created them." It is obviously time for us to shift to a different level of thinking: a new level that does not entail mindlessly adopting other theories and strategies but rather encourages us to develop our own, with consideration and awareness of all other available insights.

We have to understand that no person, party, country, or continent can be the leader forever. Existence is based on circular moves, and everything shifts as time progresses. Instead of continuing to hold on to the "bigger, better, faster" mindset, we should start thinking of the circles.

We have a challenge on our hands in teaching others—especially the older generations—that the idea of "success" is changing and that there is more to this concept than merely financial goals. It is time for us to realize that things happen for a reason and mask hidden meanings, and that by trying to detect and understand these lessons we will be uplifted and all can prosper.

References

Dewy, Russell A. "Theory Z." *Psychology: An Introduction.* 2007. Accessed Oct. 9, 2010. http://www.psywww.com/intropsych/ch09_motivation/theory_z.html

Kipling, Rudyard. "The Ballad of East and West." Accessed Oct. 9, 2010. http://www.readbookonline.net/readOnLine/2736/

"Maslow's Theory Z." Accessed Oct. 9, 2010. http://www.abraham-maslow.com/m_motivation/Theory_Z.asp

Ouchi, William. "Theory Z." Accessed Oct. 9, 2010. http://www.williamouchi.com/book_theoryz.html

Runes, Dagobert D. "Leibniz, Gottfried Withelm." *Dictionary of Philosophy.* 1942. Accessed Oct. 9, 2010. http://www.ditext.com/runes/l.html

John Krysko is president of Tri-Unity Consulting, Inc., which focuses on assisting individuals and small businesses with realizing their financial goals. To this end John has synthesized his almost 30 years as a financial planner with his lifelong interest in cross-cultural practical applications of self-actualization. In the seventies and eighties he held a series of seminars on practical financial and business applications at educational settings as diverse as San Diego State University, the Esalen Center in Big Sur, the Open Center in New York City, and the Wainwright House in Wrye, NY. A resident of Westchester, NY, John serves as treasurer of his local church, president of the local chapter of the Rotary Club, and coordinator of numerous international educational grants and foundations. He is a founding board member of the Lunchbox Fund, which helps more than 1,000 children a day in South Africa pursue their dreams. He is a member of the board of the Interfaith Center of New York. John has re-embraced his passion for teaching with new seminars on "spiritual intelligence" that focus on East/West spirituality.

Chapter XIII

From Seasoned Business Renaissance Leaders to Upcoming Ones

The final chapter of this book includes highly valuable advice from 51 business leaders. They come from a variety of cultural backgrounds and are leaders in a wide variety of settings: for-profit and non-profit; small, midsize, and large organizations; local, regional, and international companies. Due to their widely diverging industries and backgrounds, these leaders bring something very valuable to this book: a perspective that reflects every aspect that future leaders will need to consider if they want to become successful in a spiritually responsible way. Some of their opinions are as a long as a chapter, while others are as short as a few words. In any case, their messages are as colorful as the human rainbow they represent and can be captured in this Native American prayer, which we also presented in our beginning chapter:

> *Do all the good you can,*
> *in all the ways you can,*
> *with all the means you can,*
> *to all the people you can,*
> *as long as you can.*

Gift to Upcoming leaders

Richard King (founder and president of King International Group, co-founder Business Renaissance Institute, and president Go-Green Solutions, Inc.):

> *Consider your responsibility in a much broader way than you currently do. A lot of business executives maintain a very narrow vision. I would like to advise all these businesspeople to start facing the fact that their company has a responsibility far beyond that bottom line, because the issues we have to address in the world*

All of the quotes in Chapter 13 are from The Business Renaissance Quarterly and used with permission of the Journal.

*today—environmental issues, hunger, security-issues, and others—
require the private sector to step up and accept them as a responsibility. Governments can't do that, and non-profits can't do that. It
is the call for businesses, because they enter places where the two
others don't. In addition, I would request for upcoming leaders to
pay more than lip service in their relationships with their employees.
Sometimes we say a lot of things, for example in our mission statements, but the execution leaves a lot to be desired. I would advise executives to be more in touch with all levels of their company. Finally, I
would encourage them to nurture a corporate culture that addresses
humanity as a whole rather than just the stockholders. We have to
get over that kind of thinking. We should emphasize the stakeholders, and not just the stockholders.*

Russ Hanlin (former president and CEO of Sunkist Growers, Inc.):

*Leadership is most rewarding and successful when it is earned.
Earn your leadership by working hard, by being there when needed,
by taking responsibility, and by creating room for others to grow.*

Gary Hickman (president of Junior Achievement of Southern California):

*Take good care of your people. If you do that, they will take
good care of you and your mission.*

Stedman Graham (chairman and CEO of S. Graham and Associates (SGA),
a management and marketing consulting firm based in Chicago):

*Many business leaders are mainly focused on being successful
financially. I would advise them to have a holistic approach to living,
and realize that work-life balance is about long-term development.
I would further like to advise them to control and understand how
to take resources and information and make them relevant to your
whole life, which is made up of many different parts of who you are.*

Malena Ruth (president and co-founder of the African Millennium Foundation):

*I don't consider myself equipped yet to give any advice, be-
cause I still have a lot to learn from all the great business leaders out
there, young and old. I would therefore like to talk with them about
how we can collectively contribute to bettering the lives of those
most in need.*

Rinaldo Brutoco (president of the World Business Academy):

My advice consists of a couple of points:

Number 1: We're not going through times that are "business as usual." We're going through an extraordinary cultural jump. Some would say we're going through a period of conscious evolution. And in a conscious evolution it's wise that we select each of our next stages. And so, if businesspeople try to do the same thing in the same way for the same reason they will not succeed in the long run, even if it appears that they do. Let me give you an example: Even if the last 10 years of leadership at General Motors was to look back and say, "Well, look how much money we made the last 10 years," I would say, "Yes, but look at what you've done to the company's profits today!"

I picked General Motors because it was, 10 years ago, the largest industrial corporation in the world. It's rapidly shrinking. And I seriously question whether it will survive intact in all of its divisions and pieces. I'm almost certain it will not. It will go through a bankruptcy or it will be pulled apart, or it will be merged, because it's just too hopelessly broken. Now, what's broken there? Well, you can say on one level what's broken at GM is the inability to see, as recently as last year, the importance of fuel-efficient vehicles. The incredible short-sightedness of relying on SUVs and trucks for profitability. GM has been continually suppressing alternative forms of motive power, because of their historical commitment to engine plants that made the internal combustion engines. GM has failed to see that they're not in the car business, they're in the personal transportation business. As such, they should have been working for the most fuel-efficient, reliable, and socially beneficial engines they could obtain in order to use them for personal transportation systems. All of these failures together provided short-term gain (e.g. GM was able to make more money on SUVs than compacts, was able to keep using the same engine plants without major retooling, etc.) but have now taken GM to where the company as we know it is not survivable for the long term. I would say that's an example of short-term thinking that appeared to be good if you looked at the financials two to three years ago, but now in hindsight you can see that was just a temporary extraction of money for short-term profitability that basically has cost the company its long-term future. It's a classic example of short-term thinking that left GM half-dead as the clearly foreseeable outcome. If you check the speeches I've given for the last five years or longer you will note that I've been saying that GM was in serious trouble and might not survive in its present form. I picked GM because in the last decade, it was the largest industrial company in the world. It isn't anymore and continues to shrink every day. Obviously, while analysts like me were speaking out, no one at GM was listening. They could have prevented what has happened. Instead, they've made their situation worse.

And when you see a guy like, let's say, Lee Raymond, who is the recently retired CEO of Exxon, you would think, "Oh well, look at what he did for Exxon. Look at the egregious profits Exxon has been making, so he must have been a success!" And yet I would say that the egregious profits that Exxon has been making are more a testament to unrestrained greed and the failure of government to protect the people than of any unique capabilities of Mr. Raymond. We all know from the Exxon Valdez incident to the present time that Exxon has made money 1) by passing the true costs of its business operations on to the public in terms of enormous environmental externality costs; and 2) by so ensnaring government that it has been given permission to make a level of profits that would have been embarrassing to the nineteenth-century robber barons of old. The world has never seen anything like the excess profits of the oil companies, which have been fostered by the U.S. government in the last five years. It's not just Exxon, although I think they have played the "ring leader" role in a lobbying and misinformation campaign that has left the planet's environment in a shambles and planetary citizens in poverty. What Exxon is doing is driving the entire planet to a non-petroleum future. So, the profits that are being extracted now are a short-term success, but will yield a long-term failure in massive proportions. These egregious profits can only accelerate the trend toward renewable fuels. We'll leave the petroleum era that much quicker, and instead of Lee Raymond and Exxon leading that movement, they've been resisting it and attempting to hold it back by paying lobbyists, by paying politicians, and in every way (legal or otherwise) that they can.

The oil companies are just like the cigarette companies in the sixties in the way they are lying to the public, lying to Congressional committees, improperly influencing government legislation (e.g., the secret "energy bill" meetings in Dick Cheney's office that no member of the pubic was allowed to attend), stonewalling the environmentalists who are attempting to mediate some of their worst excesses, paying academics to confuse the public about global warming when they know full well it is being caused in large part by burning fossil fuels, and by spending vast sums of money to confuse the public at large to accept their nefarious schemes. Sounds at lot like what the cigarette companies did. In the case of cigarettes they obtained their wealth by basically addicting people. By the way, they're still successful 3,000 times a day—3,000 new children in America become

addicted to smoking everyday. Just think about it, the absolute opposite of a conscious businessperson is the cigarette company executive because, here's the definition of a cigarette company: They kill
people for profit. That's the absolute reverse to creating profit as a
by-product from creating something society needs. Cigarette companies literally kill people for profit. That's as far outside the system of
legitimate commerce as you can go.

People like Lee Raymond at Exxon have been doing a similar
thing. They took their egregious excess profits and they used it to
invest in more politicians, and to pay more lobbyists, and to pay
more public relations people, so they can continue to spin and build
more rules in their favor. Just recently this energy bill that passed last
year, in 2005—a so-called energy bill—which has adopted more tax
breaks for oil, as if they need them. So you have this egregious accu-
mulation of wealth and profits extracted out of society almost like at
gunpoint. In fact I saw a cartoon in the paper where an oil executive
is holding a pump—you know, the handle of a pump—to the head
of a customer saying, "Pay up or else!!!" The end of a pump is almost
like the point of a gun. And this all has accelerated with greater speed
now that the petroleum era is coming to an end. Cigarette companies addict people and literally kill for a profit. Exxon has addicted a
society, like a "pusher" keeps that society addicted through a web
of distortions, lies, and highly questionable (some would say illegal)
tactics. They are literally willing to kill this planet, this beautiful blue
marble floating in the great void of space, which holds everything on
it we know and love, just to earn their excess profits.

And here's one of those curious anomalies about how the planet
may actually strike back to save itself, using the very forces of nature
that Exxon has unleashed in order to restore balance in the eco-
system. Thirty-one percent of all the refining capacity in the United
States is on the Gulf Coast. Due to global warming occurring from
the burning of the very fossil fuels Exxon has been selling, the planet
is warming. Exxon has been doing everything it can to create doubt
about the existence of global warming when in fact it's the most
widely researched scientific topic in the history of the world—there's
actually not a shred of credible conversation that global warming
isn't being caused by human intervention. Exxon has tried to confuse
the issue, so that they can keep warming the planet by the extravagant burning of oil. Unfortunately for the U.S. oil refining industry,
however, when you warm the planet you get a hotter Gulf of Mexico;
and when you get a hotter Gulf of Mexico you get more Category 5
hurricanes, which then will strike…where?…the Gulf Coast, which is

precisely where 31% of the refineries are. It appears that the oil folks are going do it to themselves! It's quite remarkable, actually.

By contrast with Exxon's conduct, I'm delighted that Chevron is just now opening a wind farm on the island of Maui and is in conversations to become a major producer of wave energy. I'm also pleased that BP knows that it has to move "Beyond Petroleum" and is attempting to do so, particularly with its photovoltaic division. These examples demonstrate that the oil companies could choose to see themselves as "energy companies" rather than "oil companies" and by so doing could form the basis of the future of renewable energy systems which clearly will be running the planet in the very near future. It is a business renaissance person who can see what they have been is not necessarily the prescription of what they can be in the future. When they come from a business renaissance perspective I believe they will see that their own personal and corporate future will be aligned with the positive forces of change and lead to sustainable profits over the very long haul rather than excess profits, extracted at the point of the pump, in the short haul.

So, I think the answer to the question from a point of view of, what it is that I'd like to give as a way of advice is:

1. *Don't ignore the breadth of view you must have of society and commerce today if you're going to be successful. That's critical.*
2. *Recognize that the number one most valuable resource of any business, the number one stakeholder, is probably their employees. Those are the members of their extended tribe. They have to honor those employees as their principal stakeholders. They have to pay them fairly, treat them fairly, assist them with medical plans, etc.; and, they have to take care of their customers and their vendors who are also their stakeholders. If they do all those things well, all the shareholders will win, including the stakeholders called "shareholders." The shareholders will not win if they engage in the headlong short-term pursuit of profits, which is what General Motors did that caused them to end up in the place where they are now. Every farmer knows that you can't eat your seed corn. You have to be willing to preserve what's essential this quarter if you want to continue to plant and harvest next year.*

To me the advice is, look at how rapidly times are changing; there are organizations like the Academy, that are providing hundreds and hundreds of pages on subjects that can give every businessperson the breadth of knowledge they need and the opportunity to understand that breadth of knowledge within the scope of this new context we now operate from. The resources are there. Take advantage of them.

1. *There are no bystanders in the world we live in. No one is sitting in the bleachers watching. We're all on the field together. We're all interconnected. Remember that poem by John Donne:*
   No man is an island,
   Entire of itself.
   Each is a piece of the continent,
   A part of the main.
   If a clod be washed away by the sea,
   Europe is the less.
   As well as if a promontory were.
   As well as if a manner of thine own
   Or of thine friend's were.
   Each man's death diminishes me,
   For I am involved in mankind.
   Therefore, send not to know
   For whom the bell tolls,
   It tolls for thee.
   Don't ask for whom the bell tolls;
   it tolls for thee.

We are all interconnected. And therefore, what happens to the least of our brothers—if you will—is happening to us. There are implications.

1. *This is a big one: If you're very successful in business sometimes you get comfortable to the point where you think of yourself as being in the penthouse or owner's suite of this incredible ocean liner. And you get to this point where you think you're invulnerable because you're in the penthouse suite of this extraordinary ocean liner. And you don't stop and ask yourself, "Is the name of the ship Titanic?" And if it is, are you really better off because you're in the owner's suite? Or would you be better off helping to detect where that iceberg is, and helping your shipmates to avoid it? Can you just party and satiate yourself with materialistic wealth and materialistic success? Or are you better off saying, "Wait, I could help figure out where the icebergs are, because I'm good at that and I might not be able to take that one next trip on my private jet airplane; I may miss out on that next gold plate dinner, or that next extravagant vacation; but if I can detect*

a couple of social icebergs along the way, this ship just might not go down with me onboard"? At the end of the day there is no good cabin on the Titanic, no matter how rich or powerful you are, or how much you think you're in control, there's no good cabin on the SS Titanic—not even the owner's suite.

Bucky Fuller stirred a similar concept when he coined the phrase Spaceship Earth. That's what we're on here, Spaceship Earth. Business leaders must recognize that there may be a small fire in the galley halfway back in the steering section of our rocket, but if that fire burns uncontrolled, our rocket will be destroyed. We'll be lost in space. There is no such thing as a small fire in the middle of the universe. We're not taking care of the planetary substance: the air, water, temperature, coral reefs, forests, mammals, and animals. We're not taking care of it. It's like we're believing that failure to maintain our ecosystem is, perhaps, only a "small fire." As noted earlier, however, there are no "small fires" on a spaceship. In the process of eroding our natural environment we're dangerously exposing ourselves as our spaceship goes hurtling through this enormous void called the universe. And so far there's no other spaceship we can jump on when we get through messing this one up. In many places it is unsafe to drink the water or eat the plants on this planet. In every place, it is no longer safe to walk in the sunshine. In every place, we are beginning to feel the effects of a rapidly destabilizing weather situation, which is increasingly wreaking havoc and killing tens of thousands (soon this will be millions) of our planetary shipmates.

So I say to businesspeople, consider your own enlightened self-interest. Be enlightened! Your self-interest is broader than you know. And to work with that self-interest you have to have this broad set of data, you need to know about this paradigm shift, you have to have this broad macro view; you have to be willing to execute it on the micro level; to do that you have to be willing to ask questions you haven't asked and to see integration in relationships like you've never integrated before, and apply all your old skills and then some. And if you do all that, with the grace of God, we might just get through this whole thing with a minimum of pain.

Right now I think the business community is the pivotal element that will determine the amount of collective societal pain we will experience as we transition between paradigms. Our responsiveness in the business community to the trying times we live in will directly determine the amount of pain society collectively goes through to get from here to there. And I believe it's our duty, as the most powerful institution on the planet, to minimize that pain. I think that any sentient being that can watch another human writhing in pain, and not offer to help to reduce that pain, has become some sort of monster. We can no longer tolerate that we're willing to stand back as businesspeople with the leadership, the power, the strength, and the ability we have, and not take action.

I'd like to end on a positive note: Bill Gates did a lot of things building his company that a lot of people thought were immoral, unethical, and illegal, for a very long period of time. For many years Microsoft was referred to in Silicon Valley as "the evil empire." So, Bill Gates, who's not exactly a person that anybody would trust in his early Microsoft years, but who has now turned into the perfect example of how it's never too late for salvation. Bill Gates has decided that he's going to take his tremendous intelligence, which frankly is more valuable than his money, along with his money, and his commitment—this man has tremendous commitment and tremendous discipline and he's going to take that and instead of satiating himself, which is exactly what I mentioned earlier in this interview, he's going to try to identify the iceberg and help eliminate the threat. That he would do that is the most extraordinary example that I'd like to leave for other businesspeople.

So my words of advice to businesspeople are, be a Bill Gates. If you can't give up your business entirely, you don't have to. Just give up 10% of your profits. If you can't put 100% of your time in the non-profit sector, put as much as you can but at least give it some. What Bill Gates is doing now, so well is that he is becoming an example for the rest of us. And I'm not overlooking any of what he did in his earlier career. It's just not relevant because that was yesterday and this is today. And what he's been doing for the last two years is really extraordinary. He's been setting a new paradigm model for the rest of business leadership. And for that we should be extraordinarily grateful.

That Warren Buffet, the most sophisticated financial investor of our era, the second-wealthiest man in the world behind Mr. Gates, would choose to say to his own children, "I don't believe in dynastic wealth. You're all going to be comfortable, but the vast portion of my wealth I am leaving to Bill Gates to use, because he's so talented, he'll figure out how to best spend it. And that's what I need to do for the planet." That's an extraordinary example. No wonder they call him the Sage of Omaha. What an example! Now, Bill is willing to do the work and spend the money. Warren said, you know, Bill is doing the work so I'll give him the money. Every businessperson I know should duplicate at least one, and preferably both, of those examples. But they should at least say, if they're not going to lead the planet to the place where we create heaven on earth, then go find the most capable businesspeople you know, and have them do it with your resources. Because if you do that we will create a combined effect that will make a difference. It will make THE *difference.*

To paraphrase Barbara Marx Hubbard, "If we really are in a state of conscious evolution, which is the culmination of 14 billion years to this moment, it's incredibly important that we provide in business the leadership to choose for life because species in crisis over that 14 billion year period either evolve or die. We have equally the power of self-extinction or the power to create the next level of evolution."

Finally, in all the years I've been in business I have never heard of or seen any problem that exists today that we don't currently have all the technology and resources to solve. *So if we don't create a world where 38,000 children don't have to die each day, if we don't stop that needless slaughter of innocents,* think what that's saying about us a civilization. *Remember, we have all the resources, and we have all the technology we need! –– So now it's time to recognize that we can no longer sit on the sidelines. There's nobody in the bleachers. We're all on the field together. We're the business leadership at this time on the planet and it's our job is to see to it that of the two choices facing us at this moment of conscious evolution, we choose to create heaven on earth. There's no question we're totally capable of doing it. And frankly, we'll all enjoy the process. The alternative is to continue to pursue the ideologies of the prior millennia, an eye for an eye, a tooth for a tooth, ands what it will look like is Lebanon. As Gandhi observed, if we hold to the ideology of an eye for an eye and a tooth for a tooth, we will end up living in a blind and toothless society. That's where it leads, and it doesn't matter who's right or wrong. If we continue to pursue the ideologies of four millennia ago, we'll continue to see starvation, malnutrition, and lack of access to health care, food, or water. And if we proceed to pursue headlong materialism, we will succeed in creating a climate that's unlivable. So, we have all these choices, and it really is up to us. And particularly is it up to business leadership, because we have more power than any institution at this time in history. I personally believe we will choose to create heaven on earth. Nothing less would be fitting as a tribute to the enormous 14 billion year period of evolution that lead to this point compels the choice to assist humanity to jump to the next level of conscious evolution. In the sage words of Marilyn Ferguson, "Our past is not our potential." Our potential, unlike our past, is truly unlimited and will be defined exclusively by the choices we make.*

Yoshito "Super" Yamaguchi (former main executive for Mitsubishi Electronics in the United States (MELCO), current advisor to MELCO, chairman of the board of directors at Kwassui Women's College and School in Nagasaki):

> *Life is what your God planned for you. Business is the most exciting and integrated task we are given. Do it with joy and with curiosity.*

Kathleen Stillwell (president of SQM Consulting Group, and is a recognized industry expert in health care risk management, insurance, and quality management):

> *Be present in the moment. Do not wait to live; do not wait one more day to show kindness, concern, and compassion to your fellow man. Listen more than you speak, reach out to others, and encourage those around you to be all they can be. Devote time to study subjects outside your area of expertise, develop strategies to build your value system into your life and your work. To the best of your ability avoid negative people and never use your position and authority to intimidate or undermine others. Practice the power of positive thinking and recognize the strength of positive energy. Do not dwell on the past, look forward, and do what you can to leave the world a better place.*

William (Bill) Herren (founder and president of American Vision Windows, Inc.):

> *Keep your focus on serving others. Look towards God as the standard to follow, instead of following the world. The world has a low standard in regards to values and ethics. But God is faithful to provide guidelines for success, not only for your business, but your life as well. If you have a problem with the bottom line, ask yourself, "What are we not doing for our customers/employees?"*

Mei-Lee Ney (president of Richard Ney & Associates, Asset Management, Inc.):

> *Good leadership comes through setting a good example.*

Lawrence G. Shoaf (senior vice president of Aon Risk Services):

> *First, focus on people and helping them achieve their goals. This applies to managers who are leading people; CEOs who are working with their boards; and executives who are meeting with clients and prospects. If you can help these individuals achieve their goals, you will also generate greater productivity, cooperation and new business.*

Secondly: Attitude. Nothing is more critical to continued success than attitude. You have a choice each morning regarding your attitude and the choice you make will, to a very large extent, determine your success and your happiness.

Eddie Wang (president of GLC Enterprises, LLC, and Glorious Land Company, LLC (GLC)):

Don't forget that ultimately everything you do is for other people. Nowadays it is ever more important to realize that the people you service are spread out all over the globe. Therefore, instead of being only task-oriented for the short term, you should always focus on the long term in all of your decisions.

Fred Claire (former executive vice president of the LA Dodgers):

First and foremost, recognize the opportunity that you have as a leader. Recognize the opportunity and the responsibility. Do your job with the thought in mind that at the end of every day your work will withstand the close examination of others and you will have a sense of pride in the manner in which you conducted yourself. Understand that in business there are no "small things." Everything you do is important—everything you say, every action you take and the manner in which you carry out your responsibilities. And nothing is more important than your relationship with other people. Ultimately, you will be judged by these relationships. When you make a move ask yourself, "How will this look under the closest inspection? Will I take pride in how I handled this? How will I feel about this the next day, or the next year, or the next decade once everything has come to light?" If your decisions are based with these thoughts in mind you have an excellent chance of making good decisions.

Jing Jin (founder and managing director of Los Angeles-based Turnkey Capital, LLC):

The world has been undergoing significant changes. Many of the fundamental assumptions on the way we live, how we relate to the environment and conduct business have been seriously questioned. The world today calls for a paradigm shift in many fundamental aspects of our human society, and demands leaders who come forth to lead us through this critical period. We can no longer turn away from the increasing conflicts between growth, consumption, and our environment. Can we, as business leaders, lead by example and unify our people to create sustainable businesses and communities?

Dr. Sanford M. Shapero (former president and CEO of the City of Hope National Medical Center):

For me: a business Decalogue…

1. *Try new ideas or approaches even if they don't work as you envisioned. You learn from each experience.*
2. *Build teams, love and respect them, and always share the honors that your organization might confer on you.*
3. *Be humble. Most CEOs don't own the company. They serve at the discretion (sometimes whim) of others.*
4. *Always state the truth.*
5. *Always prepare. Do your homework…whether it be a speech or a business plan.*
6. *Remember always…Listen to the customer or volunteers…They are the company or institution.*
7. *Again, always show appreciation for the team you have molded. They make it all happen. In their reflected glory you will always be greater than you really are!*
8. *Your reputation and your word are the most precious assets you have. Don't squander this gift.*
9. *We always have a choice. Being truthful and ethical is morally and spiritually rewarding…but sometimes fraught with danger. Some choose monetary rewards and status. This sometimes taints your soul forever. The hard choice is truth, but worth the effort and sacrifice.*

We accomplish nothing by ourselves. Whatever spiritual force we accept has inspired us and guided us. Acknowledge that spirituality always.

Craig Hodgetts (architect, trial designer, scholar, and founding dean of the California Institute of the Arts):

Try as hard as you can to unlock the creative potential of your friends, associates, and employees. Remember that in a pluralistic world there are many paths to success open to an equal number of travelers, and that you don't have to be the only person at the top to enjoy the view.

Tammy and João Huang-Anacleto (founders and presidents of College Launch, Inc.):

Focus on your physical, mental, and spiritual health and inspire others to do the same by becoming the example that family, friends, and community notice through your actions instead of words. While going through this process, please mentor another business leader to do the same. After all, we are all students.

Roy Aaron (mediator, arbitrator, and business consultant):

Try, and then try even harder, not to hurt your employees or team members who can't really defend themselves. I have few regrets, but those I have all relate to incidents when I either mistreated or disappointed someone. It is so easy to be angry or mean to an employee or associate who disappoints you, and so difficult to mend an unintended hurt. Of course it's often necessary to discipline or even terminate an employee who can't measure up. But how you do it is what distinguishes a caring leader from a brute. Brutes lose respect very quickly.

Joan Marshall (executive director of the Pacific Asia Museum in Pasadena, CA):

My advice is to be open to new ideas, keep learning and evolving; be a good listener, show up for your staff, lead by example, and seek out advice when you need it. Look for the opportunities that life brings you.

Greg Lampert (founder and president of Liquiddium Capital Partners):

Never lose sight of the fact that no matter what type of organization you are running, it is really all about the people! They are the ones that make things happen and they have the ability to deliver a quality product or service to the client. Be self-confident but not arrogant. Teach by doing. Lead by example. The best reward is when your protégé gets your job when you move on. That is the ultimate compliment and recognition of a job well done.

Juanita Coleman-Merritt (former ombudsperson for Local District 8 of the Los Angeles Unified School District (LAUSD), and current educational consultant):

Business and organizational leaders need to remember that organizations are collectives of people and positive relationships are the foundation of sustained productivity—as I interpret Covey, we must attend as much to our capacity to produce—the goose, as we do to production itself—the egg. Staff development should be aimed at skills for building relationships as well as the operational aspects of the work.

Judi Neal (president of Neal & Associates and director of the Tyson Center for Faith and Spirituality in the Workplace at the Sam M. Walton College of Business, University of Arkansas):

1. *Do what brings you joy. Life is too short to live any other way. It is not irresponsible. In fact it's the most responsible thing you can do because then other people can emulate you and live their lives in joy. If everyone lived this way, we would all be of service to each other, we would not have to operate out of pain or a sense of lack, and we would not have to fall into the traps of control, greed, and fear.*

2. *Be as trusting as you can be. In every moment you can choose to be trusting or choose to be fearful. Trust opens up possibilities and mitigates the need for controls, bureaucracy, and gigantic policy manuals that deaden the human soul. Organizations that operate on higher trust have more energy free to be creative, innovative, and service-oriented.*

3. *Take time to be in nature. We spend most of our lives in metal cars or cement and glass buildings, and that diminishes our energy. We are a part of nature, and being in nature renews us and inspires us. This is one of the reasons businesses should commit to environmental sustainability. And more corporate training and development, and even business meetings, should take place outdoors!*

4. *Take on or deepen some kind of contemplative practice, even if it is only for a few minutes a day. Our monkey-minds get so out of control, and we so often operate out of habit, without thinking. By meditating, journaling, or practicing tai chi or yoga, we disrupt the monkey-mind and have the opportunity to touch a quieter place that allows us to break the spell that our work and busy lives so often puts us in. Out of this quietness can come some of our best ideas and insights.*

5. *See work as a spiritual teacher. Up until very recently, if someone was interested in a more spiritual life, they needed to leave everything they knew and go off to a monastery, ashram, or desert cave. Something has shifted in human consciousness, and a growing number of people are interested in growing spiritually in the midst of everyday life—and this is probably the most difficult spiritual path of all. Leaders have constant opportunities to practice love, compassion, kindness, and forgiveness in the workplace. How about being non-judgmental? Or seeing oneself as a servant leader?*

6.	*Finally, find yourself a group of like-minded leaders where you can safely let down your hair and can be authentic about your personal and professional challenges, and your visions. We are currently creating a CEO forum in conjunction with the United Nations where chief executives can come together in conversation with other leaders who want to make a difference in the world. There are many other groups like this that are similar, and it's not to hard to create your own.*

In summary, Business Renaissance leaders are those who can see what others cannot yet see, and who are willing to trust their instincts in the face of no agreement. They have been called to do something powerful in the world, and sometimes at great personal cost, they respond. Not to do so would be to sell their souls. They are not willing to do that, and we need more leaders like this in the world. And the beautiful thing is that these leaders are passionate about developing other people to be this same kind of leader. And that's how the world will change!

Kenneth R. Nielsen (president of Woodbury University):

Respect every human being for their contributions to the goals and objectives of the organization. Listen carefully to the needs and respond with action-packed programs and vision for the future. Attitude is one of the most important determining factors for achieving human success. Care about each and every individual for his or her contributions to the ultimate objectives. Enjoy your life personally and professionally. Hard work has always been the key to success, and enjoying what you are doing will lead to greater personal and professional satisfaction.

Tami Simon (founder of Sounds True, in Boulder, CO, a multimedia publishing company dedicated to disseminating spiritual wisdom):

Make sure the business you are in is truly serving the real needs of people and society not just the financial needs of stockholders. Use your business skills to make money solving real social problems.

Jacqueline Miller (executive producer and co-creator of the World Voice™ Concert and president/co-founder of Partnerships for Change (PFC), a San Francisco-based nonprofit (or social-profit, as the immediate stakeholders prefer to call it) 501c3 organization dedicated to positive transformation at the community level):

Advice for other business executives:

- *Lead with your heart; who cares the most will win.*
- *Do sustainable development with love that improves the lives of everyone involved in your entire global supply chain.*
- *Leave footprints on the hearts of those you have served not on the earth you have abused.*

Halilu Haruna (CEO of Bali Business Management, Inc., a corporation focused on financial planning, financial control, and analysis):

The advice I want to give to business leaders is that they need to be more caring and sensitive to their clients' needs and make sure the clients they serve are successful. Once your clients are successful there is no limit to your success. When you are caring you stand out, and the profits will come when you do what you do successfully.

Mashi Rahmani (founder and CEO of MMC, Inc., a pioneer in the human resources outsourcing/consulting industry):

First, remain humble at heart but continue to push yourselves toward greater horizons and personal development. Second, I believe learning is a lifelong activity—embrace this concept of a true Renaissance individual. Additionally, I believe constant innovation is what separates businessmen/businesswomen and future leaders. Lastly, I would advise business leaders to develop their own spiritual well-being—this has been one of my most significant personal strategies that has propelled me toward both career success and personal content.

Dr. Timothy A. Kelly (former director of the DePree Center Public Policy Institute, currently a consultant in China):

I have come to believe that there are two mistakes often made by gifted, motivated people in their pursuit of excellence. The first is to become isolated, to trust no one, to rely only on oneself. This can work in the short run, but eventually leads to a bitter and lonely existence that robs the joy of life and limits one's effectiveness as a business leader. The alternative is to decide to have a balanced life, including time with friends and family, even if that means tolerating some lost opportunities. The leader who is balanced in this way will tend to make better decisions for the organization, and will last longer!

The second mistake is to ignore the spiritual dimension of life altogether, usually because there is "just no time." As someone once said, What is the point of gaining the whole world but losing your soul? The alternative is to explore the mystery of life, wrestle with questions of meaning, and seek spiritual understanding. This leads not only to a more mature personality—one with gravitas—but also to greater effectiveness as a leader. Followers can sense when their leader is shallow, and respect one who is thoughtful and authentic.

Walter Rose (founding partner of Venture Consulting Corp. (VCC)):

My advice to business leaders:

1. *Recognize your unique opportunity to motivate people to accomplish more than they believe capable of doing by themselves.*
2. *Work to understand the points of view of others in your organization, and give them the confidence that their input is important to you.*
3. *Trust your instincts with your employees but verify decisions with data and analysis.*

Strive for what my business school professor called "goal congruence" to energize the organization as a whole to move to a higher level of performance.

Thomas E. Higgins (chairman of Higgins, Marcus & Lovett, Inc.):

Don't listen to the experts. Become the expert.

Dr. Margaret Benefiel (CEO of Executive Soul Business Consultancy Firm, past president of the spirituality and religion department of the Academy of Management, and lecturer at Andover Newton Theological School in Boston and at the Milltown Institute in Dublin, Ireland):

In this economy, you may want to play it safe and focus only on the bottom line. That approach will kill your business. Take the risk of leading from your soul. You'll be amazed at how your organization will thrive.

Nem Bajra (co-founder and president at Calsoft Systems):

I would highly recommend building a corporate culture together with employees.

Dr. Barbara Miner (psychotherapist and self-improvement and spiritual consultant):

Relax. Be yourself. Follow your own highest call, and don't worry about what comes next. We do not ever know what is coming next, so worrying about it is senseless, as well as counterproductive.

When the leader relaxes and follows their vision or their own highest call, others can relax and do the same. Together you can become a powerful force toward a business, which supports that which what is highest in the human's spirit.

Products, services, and ideas can all serve to support what advances human sensibilities. All it requires is a vision, action toward that vision, engaging the collective aspirations and support of our colleagues, and taking that step toward what we feel called to accomplish on the behalf of what is positive for all.

Tomonori Ishii (senior vice president and general manager of the Americas for All Nippon Airways):

Explore the bottom-up management style, encourage a work environment that allows your staff to communicate with you directly and candidly. The more you know about the challenges your frontline employees face, the better you will be equipped to collaborate on effective solutions. And you will avoid becoming the emperor with no clothes.

Dr. Carol Soucek King (author and founder of The Institute of Philosophy & the Arts):

That we might do everything we can to make this world a better place—to reflect our inherent being-ness in harmony and love, and our knowledge that every single aspect of life and work is interconnected with every other aspect. That means we are vitally interconnected with every person with whom we have contact—and even with every person with whom we have no visible contact. It means we are interconnected with every living being and every single thing. Therefore, since we have such a little time on this earth—to the greatest extent possible, we must choose the way of expectant joy and positive uplifted thought. We must soar onward in our lives and work on the wings of gentle kindness.

Richard Barrett (founder and chairman of Barrett Values Centre and author and consultant):

Find out what your soul is asking you to do or what you are passionate about, and do it.

Edgar Johnson (president and CEO of Johnson Enterprises):

Understand what makes others tick and you will be successful.

Cathy Winch (general manager of The B.L. Winch Group, Inc., which houses two publishing imprints, Personhood Press and Jalmar Press):

> *I don't offer advice, just a thought. Vision, courage, perseverance, and personal accountability will forge tremendous change in the current state of corporate and business affairs. Be the change you wish to see.*

John H. Quinn (president and CEO of PROMÉRICA BANK):

> *Engage passionately in your endeavors. Know what is expected of you and what you yourself want to accomplish. Communicate well with others up and down the line, helping them understand the issues and the solutions, what you will do and will not do. Clarity of purpose and understanding the "why" of the organization and individual efforts is a key to success. Keeping people in balance, happy and motivated. If they are not these things, they will not perform to potential. Have fun.*

Ananth Natarajan (physician-entrepreneur and co-founder and former CEO of Infinite Biomedical Technologies (IBT)):

> *I would recommend surrounding yourself with others who share your passion and core values. Furthermore, when considering allowing someone to have a stake in your company, be sure to consider not just the financial implications but also the effect on the mission of the organization.*

Dr. Joan Marques (co-founder of Business Renaissance Institute (BRI) and Academy of Spirituality and Professional Excellence (ASPEX), author, educator, and social entrepreneur):

> *This might not necessarily be advice, rather a suggestion: ask yourself if what you are doing today is what you would still do if you could do it all over again. If not, start devoting some more time to the things you feel good about. It is never too late to shift your paradigm and, subsequently, your actions. Adults in our times go through an average of three careers. The best career is the one where you find gratification, and know at the same time, that you are doing something good for society. Today is a great day for a start.*

Dr. Marshall Goldsmith (author, educator, renowned management thinker, and consultant):

> *This is actually a piece of advice that I have for people in general. My best advise is to take a deep breath, imagine that you're 95*

years old and you're on your deathbed: you are getting ready to die. But right before you're taking your last breath, you're given a wonderful gift: the ability to go back in time and talk to the person who is reading this message. What advice would the wise 95-year-old you, who knows what was really important in life, and what wasn't, what mattered and what didn't, what counts and what doesn't, have for the you that is reading this message right now? How about taking a breath and thinking about that? This is professional as well as personal advice. Whatever you are thinking right now, my advice is, do that.

Dr. Deborah DiCessare (dean of academic affairs and economic development at Los Angeles Valley College):

Today's rapidly changing times require a leadership revolution. We need to lead people through the nobility of our own character; therefore, we need to develop our own character first. As leaders, we need to expand our capacities on every level. More than ever we need to be strong, confident, true to one's beliefs, maintain high aspirations and fix our eye on the universal picture, take initiative, be tenacious and flexible, and have keen insight into human character. We must be willing to listen to others, ask thought-provoking questions, and thank colleagues for their contributions. Never rest on our laurels; never lose hope. Remember we win through wisdom not bureaucracy. We need to maintain a global perspective recognizing our world's increasing interdependence.

Don St. Clair (vice president for marketing at Woodbury University and educator in organizational leadership):

Find your own style and be true to yourself. It's good to study successful leaders to learn from their styles and actions. Ultimately though, to be effective, you have to do it from within your own skin. I believe authenticity to be the single most important leadership quality. Authenticity is pure. It's admitting that you are not perfect and striving to achieve within your own being. Only when you are able to do that for yourself, can you help others do the same.

Pegi Matsuda (publisher and president of the *San Fernando Valley Business Journal*):

Ask questions, listen and get to know your employees. You'll be pleasantly surprised at what you learn. Don't be afraid to ask your employees for advice and opinions—many employees are waiting for an invitation to engage in the process. Treat your customers with the respect they deserve and look for ways to know your customers better. Don't take customers for granted and always apologize when you make a mistake.

Dr. Masayoshi "Mike" Yamano (president and chairman of the board of Yamano Gakuen, president of Yamano International Beauty Association, chancellor of the Yamano College of Aesthetics, principal of Yamano Japanese Language School, and principal of Yamano Medical College):

> *Study. Be prepared. Lucky things may come along, but the important thing is that, when lucky things come along, you must be prepared to grab them. So I would tell those who wish to be good business leaders, read a lot and be ready—be ready to catch your "luckies." Otherwise, those opportunities will pass you by—and you will not even know it!*

Sandy Bleifer (artist and activist in community involvement, focusing on revitalization of L.A.'s Central City):

> *Share your knowledge and experience with people just starting. Sure, we all learn by experience, but that learning curve can be a killer. Having a mentor contributes to the survival rate.*

Dr. Satinder Dhiman (co-founder Business Renaissance Institute and Academy of Spirituality and Professional Excellence and professor of management and associate dean of Woodbury University School of Business, Burbank, CA):

> *My suggestions to other business leaders would be to focus more on self-development, self-awareness, and self-knowledge. When leaders go astray, it is almost always a case of failure of personal leadership. So, one has to start very near, i.e., with one's own self. Leadership has been defined as a journey into one's soul. I could not agree more.*
>
> *It is important to remember that the journey from success to significance (and from happiness to peace and harmony) is not only essential for personal mastery, it is also critical in developing and leading others.*
>
> *I would like to end my contribution by briefly summarizing what I call Seven Habits of Highly Fulfilled Leaders. These are approached as seven gifts or seven offerings that highly fulfilled leaders share with others. The good news is that when we give these gifts to others, we end up receiving much more blessings in return. To quote Emerson:*

"It is one of the most beautiful compensations of life that no man can sincerely try to help another without helping himself."

These gifts are:

1. *The Gift of Pure Motivation*
2. *The Gift of Gratitude*
3. *The Gift of Generosity*
4. *The Gift of Harmlessness*
5. *The Gift of Total Acceptance*
6. *The Gift of Selfless Service*
7. *The Gift of Presence*

Pure motivation signifies that whatever we do, our intention behind every action should be motivated by our desire to help, to benefit others, without expecting anything in return. *The gift of gratitude is our resounding tribute of appreciation to the entire universe. This gift springs from a deep realization that our whole life depends on the kindness of others. In fact, the whole universe has to participate or collaborate to make our existence possible. By being grateful, we also open our hearts to receive more that is still to come our way. When we truly understand this, we begin to move away from the right of entitlement to the realm of responsibility and our actions become true expressions of deep gratitude and thankfulness. The gift of generosity flows directly from the gift of gratitude. Through this gift we share our bounties with others as a direct expression of our gratitude towards the universe. Churchill is reported to have said, "We make a living by what we get, but we make a life by what we give." Again, we have to check our motivation here. Is it pure, or do we have our own axe to grind under the guise of generosity?*

The gift of harmlessness is born out of our understanding of the previous gifts. When all of our actions are inspired by pure motivation and when we are mindful of our great gratitude for everything and for everyone, we gently come upon the gift of harmlessness towards the entire universe. The gift of harmlessness goes much deeper than non-harming in the physical sense. It includes non-harming by thought, by speech, and by action. Just imagine how different things would be if a few members of a community take a vow of harmlessness. Just imagine how different our workplaces will be if a small fraction of its members decide to live by the principle of harmlessness. And just imagine how much peace we can foster if we can elevate this gift to a macro level.

The gift of total acceptance ultimately means accepting ourselves as we are and accepting others as they are. As long as there is any aspiration to become something different than what we are, life remains a struggle. By relinquishing the need to be different than what we are, we step out of the cycle of becoming and enter into the peaceful abode of being, which is always available to us in the present. Being yourself involves no struggle; it is the most easiest and natural thing in life and requires no time. It is always available to us right here and now, effortlessly. As long as we remain trapped in the cocoon of resentment and blame, there is no possibility of any real peace and happiness. So, the real secret of bringing true peace and harmony in our relationship—personally and professionally, is just this: total acceptance—accepting ourselves as we are and accepting others as they are.

The gift of selfless service is a natural flowering of the previous gifts. When one truly understands the gift of gratitude, the gift of generosity and the fact of interconnectedness of all life, one devotes oneself in finding joy in selfless service. As Albert Schweitzer put it so eloquently, "I don't know what your destiny will be, but one thing I know: the only ones among you who will be really happy are those who have sought and found how to serve." And, finally, the gift of true presence. As leaders, the best gift we can give others is the gift of our presence, our attentive listening, our empathy, our kindness, caring, and compassion. This is possible only if we are truly present in all our engagements and interactions. Our true nature is of the nature of "wisdom seeking wisdom." And this wisdom is always available to all of us right here and right now, whenever and wherever we need it, if only we open ourselves to it.

Paradoxically, in sharing these gifts with others, we ultimately bestow them on ourselves. As a Chinese saying goes: "A little perfume stays with the hand that gives flowers to others." Thanks for the opportunity to share my musings.

John Krysko (president of Tri-Unity Consulting, Inc.):

Listen to your inner-heart and follow it with the utmost diligence and greatest intelligence in your business practice. Continue to cultivate your own growth and those whom you meet in the workplace. This is perhaps said best by the Chinese philosopher Mencius (371-289 BCE): "Every duty is a charge, but the charge of oneself is the root of all others."

Fran Inman (principal at Majestic Realty Co., one of the nation's largest privately held, family-owned real estate development companies):

Walk the walk, listen well, focus on the tasks at hand and don't get bogged down by the external chatter, and never forget to give back.

R. Morgan Harwith (executive vice president of ClearWater Holdings, Ltd.):

I'm more focused on what I'm doing for my own business than in advising other business leaders. If I can live right, others may feel free to adopt. My advice to myself includes:

- *Develop business opportunities that give local people the opportunity to control their own lives. When there is locally produced energy, people have a basic tool to create new business opportunities that improve local living conditions.*
- *We all live on Mother Earth, and have a responsibility to take care of it. Do the right thing.*
- *There are consequences to all of our actions. Do your best to consider these consequences in advance.*
- *What are you doing to develop the people who work with you?*
- *We live in a global market. Live like there are no secrets.*